Getting Started with nopCommerce

An in-depth, practical guide to getting your first
e-commerce website up and running using
nopCommerce

Brandon Atkinson

[PACKT] PUBLISHING

open source
community experience distilled

BIRMINGHAM - MUMBAI

Getting Started with nopCommerce

First published: June 2013

Production Reference: 1280513

Published by Packt Publishing Ltd.
Livery Place
35 Livery Street
Birmingham B3 2PB, UK.

ISBN 978-1-78216-644-3

www.packtpub.com

Cover Image by Jarek Blaminsky (milak6@wp.pl)

Credits

Author
Brandon Atkinson

Reviewers
Nicholas Cipollina

Jennie Cook

Chris Stout

Acquisition Editor
Andrew Duckworth

Comissioning Editor
Neha Nagwekar

Technical Editors
Vrinda Nitesh Bhosale

Dominic Pereira

Project Coordinator
Amey Sawant

Proofreader
Paul Hindle

Indexer
Monica Ajmera Mehta

Production Coordinator
Shantanu Zagade

Cover Work
Shantanu Zagade

About the Author

Brandon Atkinson is an architect and developer for CapTech Consulting in Richmond, VA. He specializes in Microsoft technologies including ASP.NET and SharePoint, regularly contributing to the SharePoint forums on TechNet. Brandon has owned and operated several online stores over the years, and he has also helped many others with their e-commerce efforts. When he is not writing code, Brandon enjoys playing music, reading, and spending time with his wife.

This book is dedicated to my dad, Mike Atkinson. I'm sure he would be proud to see how far I've come and I miss him every day.

I thank my wife, Jennie Cook, who has always supported me in everything I do and has never told me any idea was too crazy to try; I love you.

Thanks to my brother, Brian Atkinson, who was my Sherpa guide for writing a book.

And thanks to my mom, Brenda Michaels, who taught me to have a firm hand shake, be polite, look people in the eye, and always hold doors for strangers. These skills have proven more valuable in my career than any bit of technical knowledge I can fit into my head.

About the Reviewers

Nicholas Cipollina is a Senior Software Engineer with expertise in .NET development and iOS development. He has over 12 years of software development experience including developing large-scale n-tier web applications and iOS mobile applications. Nicholas received his Bachelor of Science degree in Management Information Systems from Liberty University in Lynchburg, VA. He currently lives in Mechanicsville, VA, with his beautiful wife, Dawn, and his two little girls, Isabella and Hannah.

Jennie Cook received her Bachelor of Arts degree in Fashion Merchandising from Virginia Commonwealth University in 2004. She is a business consultant specializing in merchandising and marketing of e-commerce retail businesses and enjoys working with start-up businesses in particular.

With over 10 years of experience, Jennie amassed a wealth of knowledge that she now shares with her students as an adjunct professor in the Fashion Merchandising department at her alma mater.

Currently, Jennie is working on her own online venture using nopCommcerce. Revelry Row, a website specializing in women's jewelry and accessories, was launched in 2012.

Chris Stout is a manager at CapTech Consulting, and has spent over 15 years working on a variety of web-related technologies. He is currently working in mobile security with a financial services client, and has interest in Windows Phone development and cloud computing. When not at work, Chris enjoys woodworking, scuba diving, and hanging with his wife and daughter.

www.PacktPub.com

Support files, eBooks, discount offers and more

You might want to visit www.PacktPub.com for support files and downloads related to your book.

Did you know that Packt offers eBook versions of every book published, with PDF and ePub files available? You can upgrade to the eBook version at www.PacktPub.com and as a print book customer, you are entitled to a discount on the eBook copy. Get in touch with us at service@packtpub.com for more details.

At www.PacktPub.com, you can also read a collection of free technical articles, sign up for a range of free newsletters and receive exclusive discounts and offers on Packt books and eBooks.

http://PacktLib.PacktPub.com

Do you need instant solutions to your IT questions? PacktLib is Packt's online digital book library. Here, you can access, read and search across Packt's entire library of books.

Why Subscribe?

- Fully searchable across every book published by Packt
- Copy and paste, print and bookmark content
- On demand and accessible via web browser

Free Access for Packt account holders

If you have an account with Packt at www.PacktPub.com, you can use this to access PacktLib today and view nine entirely free books. Simply use your login credentials for immediate access.

Table of Contents

Preface

You're reading this book because you've decided to open an online store and you've chosen nopCommerce as your e-commerce engine. Congratulations! Opening an e-commerce storefront is an exciting adventure and nopCommerce is a top-shelf product that will serve you well. nopCommerce is an open source e-commerce engine built with Microsoft's ASP.NET MVC framework and which uses Microsoft's SQL Server database. This engine is a complete solution that includes everything you need.

nopCommerce consists of two major areas:

- **Public-facing storefront**: This is where customers will browse your site, look at products, and place orders. It consists of product, category, and topic pages, as well as the shopping cart and checkout pages.

- **Administration site**: This is where you will manage all aspects of your storefront. This includes creating categories, adding/managing products, and creating/editing topic pages. You will also manage shipping options, tax settings, payment providers, and so on.

There are other areas in nopCommerce, including a blog and forums. However, these areas are outside the scope of this book, but you should be aware there is more to nopCommerce than just the e-commerce engine.

Real world

In most installations, you may not use the built-in blog and forums provided. There are many products on the market that are solely built for these purposes, such as WordPress for blogging. Sometimes, it makes sense to use nopCommerce solely as your e-commerce engine and use other products for blogging and forums.

nopCommerce is licensed under the nopCommerce Public License v3. This license is the GPLv3 license with the additional requirement of having **Powered by nopCommerce** text on the bottom of each page. The GPLv3 license states that the software is free to use, change, share, and also that you are free to share your code changes with other users. Visit the GNU website (http://www.gnu.org/) for detailed information on the GPLv3 license.

The text requirement under the nopCommerce Public License v3 can be removed by purchasing a "nopCommerce copyright removal key" from the nopCommerce website.

This book was written using nopCommerce 2.80. All of the screenshots are from this version, which introduced a new theme that was not available in previous versions. However, the majority of the content is applicable to all versions of nopCommerce from 2.00 and above. To view all the versions of nopCommerce and to obtain details of the differences, visit the nopCommerce website.

What this book covers

Chapter 1, Downloading and Installing nopCommerce, will explain the various flavors of nopCommerce and will show you how to download and install the engine to your hosting provider or development environment.

Chapter 2, The Public-facing Storefront, will guide you through the storefront your customers will be using, explaining the various components along the way.

Chapter 3, The Administration Site, will guide you through the backend of nopCommerce and will highlight key areas where you'll be building your store.

Chapter 4, Configuring the Store, gives you a walkthrough of how to configure the most important areas of your store to get up and running fast.

Chapter 5, Processing Orders, will explain how to process orders you receive via your storefront as well as how to manage shipments and impersonate your customers.

What you need for this book

nopCommerce has several requirements needed before you begin working with it. These requirements and pre-requisites are different if you plan on performing custom development versus installing and using nopCommerce out of the box. The following list applies to versions of nopCommerce 2.0 through 2.8.

The following base components are required:

- Supported Operating Systems – Windows 7, Windows 8, Windows Server 2008, Windows Server 2012 (all with Internet Information Services (IIS) 7.0 or above installed).

- Supported Databases – Microsoft SQL Server 2005 or above, Microsoft SQL Server Compact 4.0 or above.

- ASP.NET 4.5 with MVC 4.

- Supported Browsers – Microsoft Internet Explorer 6.0 or above, Mozilla Firefox 2.0 or above, Google Chrome 1.0 or above, Apple Safari 2.0 or above.

- FileZilla (or other FTP software) – In order to upload your files to your hosting provider, you will need an FTP program to facilitate the transfer. You can download FileZilla from `http://filezilla-project.org/`.

- 7-Zip (or other file archive software) – When you download nopCommerce it will be in a compressed archive that will need to be extracted. You can download 7-Zip from `http://7-zip.org/`.

If you plan to write custom code or modify the code you will also need to the following:

- Microsoft Visual Studio 2012 or above

- Microsoft SQL Server 2005 or above

Who this book is for

This book is for anyone who wants to build an e-commerce website using nopCommerce. No development experience is required to use nopCommerce or for this book. If you would like to perform custom development with nopCommerce, you should have experience using Visual Studio as well as ASP.NET MVC, C#, and jQuery.

Conventions

In this book, you will find a number of styles of text that distinguish between different kinds of information. Here are some examples of these styles, and an explanation of their meaning.

Code words in text, database table names, folder names, filenames, file extensions, pathnames, dummy URLs, user input, and Twitter handles are shown as follows: "Using your FTP program, connect to your hosting provider and upload all the files from the `nopCommerce_2.80_NoSource` folder."

New terms and **important words** are shown in bold. Words that you see on the screen, in menus or dialog boxes for example, appear in the text like this: "Navigate to **Start | Control Panel | Programs**".

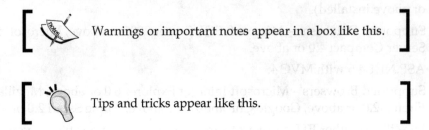

Warnings or important notes appear in a box like this.

Tips and tricks appear like this.

Reader feedback

Feedback from our readers is always welcome. Let us know what you think about this book—what you liked or may have disliked. Reader feedback is important for us to develop titles that you really get the most out of.

To send us general feedback, simply send an e-mail to feedback@packtpub.com, and mention the book title via the subject of your message.

If there is a topic that you have expertise in and you are interested in either writing or contributing to a book, see our author guide on www.packtpub.com/authors.

Customer support

Now that you are the proud owner of a Packt book, we have a number of things to help you to get the most from your purchase.

Errata

Although we have taken every care to ensure the accuracy of our content, mistakes do happen. If you find a mistake in one of our books—maybe a mistake in the text or the code—we would be grateful if you would report this to us. By doing so, you can save other readers from frustration and help us improve subsequent versions of this book. If you find any errata, please report them by visiting http://www.packtpub.com/submit-errata, selecting your book, clicking on the **errata submission form** link, and entering the details of your errata. Once your errata are verified, your submission will be accepted and the errata will be uploaded on our website, or added to any list of existing errata, under the Errata section of that title. Any existing errata can be viewed by selecting your title from http://www.packtpub.com/support.

Piracy

Piracy of copyrighted material on the Internet is an ongoing problem across all media. At Packt, we take the protection of our copyright and licenses very seriously. If you come across any illegal copies of our works, in any form, on the Internet, please provide us with the location address or website name immediately so that we can pursue a remedy.

Please contact us at `copyright@packtpub.com` with a link to the suspected pirated material.

We appreciate your help in protecting our authors, and our ability to bring you valuable content.

Questions

You can contact us at `questions@packtpub.com` if you are having a problem with any aspect of the book, and we will do our best to address it.

1
Downloading and Installing nopCommerce

nopCommerce is easy to obtain and easy to install. Whether you are a talented developer looking forward to highly customize your site, or you're a business owner who would just like to get their online store up and running fast, you'll find a flavor for you. nopCommerce can be downloaded as a ready to install e-commerce engine or as full source code ready to be modified. No matter which path you take, the end result is the same—a fully-featured e-commerce engine that will allow you to sell your products online and make money. This chapter will cover everything you need to know for downloading and installing nopCommerce. If you are interested in developing custom code, we'll also cover what prerequisites you will need and how to set up your development environment.

Prerequisites and requirements

nopCommerce has several requirements needed before you begin working with it. These requirements and prerequisites are different if you plan on performing custom development versus installing and using nopCommerce out of the box. The following list applies to versions of nopCommerce 2.0 through 2.8.

The following base components are required:

- **Supported operating systems**: Windows 7, Windows 8, Windows Server 2008, and Windows Server 2012 (all with Internet Information Services (IIS) 7.0 or above installed).
- **Supported databases**: Microsoft SQL Server 2005 or above, and Microsoft SQL Server Compact 4.0 or above.
- ASP.NET 4.5 with MVC 4.

- **Supported browsers**: Microsoft Internet Explorer 6.0 or above, Mozilla Firefox 2.0 or above, Google Chrome 1.0 or above, and Apple Safari 2.0 or above.

- **FileZilla (or other FTP software)**: In order to upload your files to your hosting provider, you will need an FTP program to facilitate the transfer. You can download FileZilla from `http://filezilla-project.org/`.

- **7-Zip (or other file archive software)**: When you download nopCommerce, it will be in a compressed archive that will need to be extracted. You can download 7-Zip at `http://7-zip.org/`.

If you plan to write custom code or modify the existing code, you will also need to install the following:

- Microsoft Visual Studio 2012 or above
- Microsoft SQL Server 2005 or above

Hosting providers

Whether you intend to use nopCommerce out of the box or you want to make changes to the code, eventually you will need to host your website so that the public can visit your site and buy your products! Hosting providers literally host your website and provide a way for users to get to your site. nopCommerce can be hosted with almost any provider that uses Windows-based servers.

Choosing a hosting provider is an important decision. There are a lot of factors that should be considered before selecting a provider. First and foremost, you'll need to ensure your provider offers Windows hosting and one of the supported operating systems and databases, and has ASP.NET 4.5 with MVC 4. In addition, the following factors should be considered:

- **Uptime**: A good provider should guarantee 99.9 percent uptime. Uptime simply means that your site will be up and running and available for users. If your site is consistently down or not available, you won't sell many products.

- **Support**: Look for providers who offer 24/7 technical support. Ideally, you want 24/7 phone support, but sometimes this can be hard to find. Look for a provider who offers phone, e-mail, and live chat support.

- **Cost**: For the most part, Windows hosting is relatively inexpensive. Choose a provider who offers annual or semi-annual discounts.

- **Dedicated IP address**: Most nopCommerce installations will require an SSL certificate as you will be processing credit cards. Check with your provider about the cost of a dedicated IP address for your domain, as it should not be a very high cost.

- **Backups**: Ensure your provider offers backups of your installation and database. This can either be automated backups or manual, but you will feel safer knowing your data has been backed up.

- **Growth options**: As your site gets more users and you make more sales, your site will need to grow as well. A good provider will offer options for growing your site, from more disk space to more database space. This would also include moving from a shared server to a dedicated server.

You can visit the nopCommerce website to view their list of Premium Partners. These are recommended hosting providers, all of which guarantee that nopCommerce can be installed and run on their servers.

Real world

Most providers offer shared hosting options at around the same price with 99.9 percent uptime. Because of this, support and growth options play a very important role in your decision. If your site goes down, you'll want to make sure that you can contact your provider immediately and get a response. Also, as your site grows you don't want to be locked into expensive upgrade options.

Setting up a basic development environment

A development environment is an area away from your public store where you can test out changes to your site. This is always a good idea if you are making user interface changes, code changes, or critical configuration changes. You can make these in your development environment without fear of affecting your public store or impacting users on your site. Once you are satisfied with the changes, you can then apply them to your public store.

A development environment is not needed to work with nopCommerce. You can instead opt to upload the files to your hosting provider and start using your site immediately. However, this is not recommended. There are a lot of settings and changes you will want to test before applying them to your public/production site.

Installing Internet Information Services (IIS)

Your development system can utilize any of the supported operating systems. However, you will most likely need to install the Internet Information Services (IIS). IIS is a web server that is used by hosting providers to run websites. It is part of Windows and you can use it to run your nopCommerce website on your PC to help develop and customize it away from your public storefront.

To install IIS, follow these steps:

1. Navigate to **Start | Control Panel | Programs**.

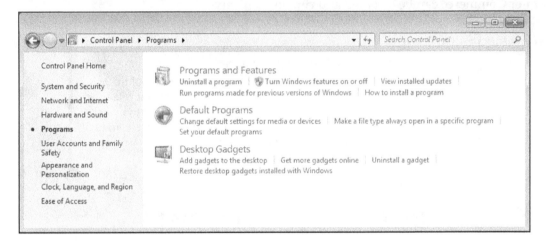

2. Click on **Turn Windows features on or off**.

3. Check the **Internet Information Services** checkbox. This will automatically check **Web Management Tools and World Wide Web Services**.

4. Click on **OK**. This will install IIS, after which you will need to restart your system.

Installing SQL Server and Visual Studio

nopCommerce requires Microsoft SQL Server, and if you plan to perform custom development, you will also need Visual Studio. Fortunately, Microsoft provides free Express versions of this software. These versions are not as feature-packed as some of their higher-end counter parts, but they are still very powerful products and will allow you to run and modify nopCommerce in your development environment.

- **SQL Server Express 2012**: This version of SQL Server is ideal for developing and powering web and small server applications. You can download this version of SQL Server from `http://www.microsoft.com/sql`.

- **Visual Studio 2012 Express for Web**: This version of Visual Studio is made for building web applications with the latest standards. You can download this version of Visual Studio from `http://www.microsoft.com/visualstudio`.

After downloading each of these products, run their installers, starting with SQL Server. After SQL Server is installed, install Visual Studio to complete your development environment.

These two products will also install the other pre-requisites needed for nopCommerce, namely ASP.NET 4.5 and MVC 4.

Downloading nopCommerce

You can download nopCommerce from the official site at `http://www.nopcommerce.com`. There are several options available when downloading nopCommerce. In order to determine which option to download, you need to decide how you will use it. The following options are available:

- **Web (no source)**: This option is available for users who do not wish/need to develop any custom code. This is a pre-compiled version of nopCommerce that can simply be uploaded to your hosting provider and used immediately. With this option, users can still modify the look and feel or user interface (UI) of their site to suit their needs, but they do not have to worry about development.

- **Source code**: This option contains a full Visual Studio solution. It is for users who wish to customize the code within nopCommerce. It contains all the source code used to develop nopCommerce and must be opened in Visual Studio. It also includes scripts to build and compile the solution to upload to your hosting provider.

- **Upgrade script**: The upgrade script option is for users who have a nopCommerce installation already in place. The script will upgrade your current installation to the latest version.

- **Microsoft Web Platform Installer**: The Web PI is a free tool from Microsoft that allows users to download software. It's a one-stop source for a wide variety of products, including nopCommerce, SQL Server Express, and Visual Studio Express. You can download nopCommerce using the Web PI directly from the nopCommerce site.

As you can see, nopCommerce can be deployed by a wide range of users with various skill sets. With each of these options, excluding the upgrade script, you can deploy nopCommerce to your development environment and your hosting provider.

Choose the option that you would like to download and click on the appropriate download link to begin your download. It is recommended that you create a new folder on your desktop to store your downloaded files for easy access.

nopCommerce will be downloaded in a compressed archive that will need to be extracted. At the time of writing, the archive is using RAR compression. If you have 7-Zip or other file archive software, you can simply right-click on the file and choose to extract the files.

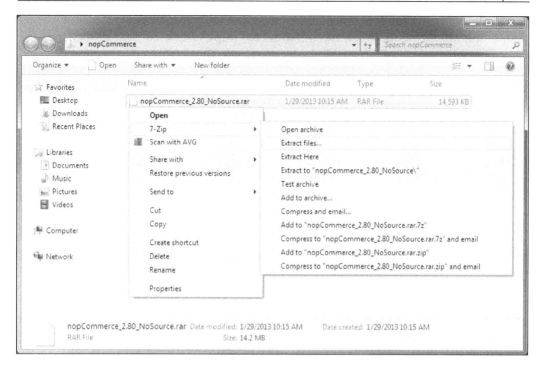

 Real world

7-Zip can open many other types of file archives including ZIP, RAR, GZIP, and TAR. It's free to download and use.

It is recommended that you choose the option that will create a new folder for you. In the case of 7-Zip, this is titled **Extract to "nopCommerce_2.80_NoSource"**. Choosing this option creates a new folder alongside the downloaded archive.

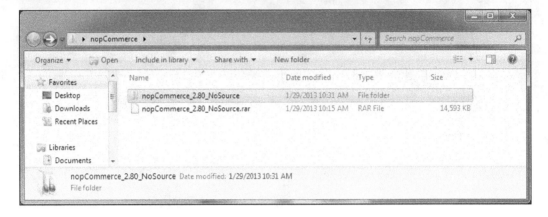

No matter which version you download, you should now have a folder that contains all the files you'll be working on.

Uploading and installing

How to install nopCommerce will depend on which version you've downloaded. In each version, the steps are very similar, but we'll look at each one separately. We'll only be looking at two of the available options, namely Web (no source) and source code. The **upgrade script** option is outside the scope of this book, as it implies you already have a previous version of nopCommerce installed. Using the Web Platform Installer is a "point and click" guided installation that is self explanatory.

In most cases, you are going to use one of the two options we'll be looking at next.

For this book, I'll be using the local IIS server in my development environment for all the examples. This means you can simply copy and paste all the files needed to the local IIS folder located at C:\inetpub\wwwroot. If you are using a development environment, you can do the same. If you chose to deploy directly to your hosting provider, you can upload your files via FTP. Once you have your hosting provider set up, you can create an FTP login and password to access your provider with.

Before uploading, you will need to create your database. Work with your hosting provider to create your database and user account. You will need to supply this information when installing nopCommerce.

Web (no source)

Deploying the Web (no source) version of nopCommerce is fairly straightforward. Your hosting account should have a `root` folder where all your web application files will be uploaded. Using your FTP program, connect to your hosting provider and upload all the files from the `nopCommerce_2.80_NoSource` folder. If you are using a development environment, simply copy all of the files and paste them to your IIS folder located at `C:\inetpub\wwwroot` (choose **Copy and Replace** if existing files are present; this will ensure the new files are copied in but existing file permissions stay intact).

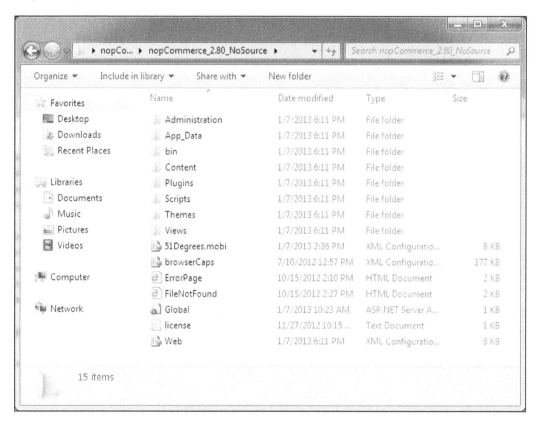

Once all the files are uploaded, open a web browser and navigate to the following URL: `http://www.YOURDOMAINNAME.com/install` (where YOURDOMAINNAME is the domain name you selected and attached to your hosting account). If you are using a development environment, navigate to `http://localhost/install`.

Source code

The Source code version of nopCommerce comes with a complete Visual Studio solution as well as scripts to build and package the website for deployment. Once you have extracted all the source files, you can run the included Deploy.bat file.

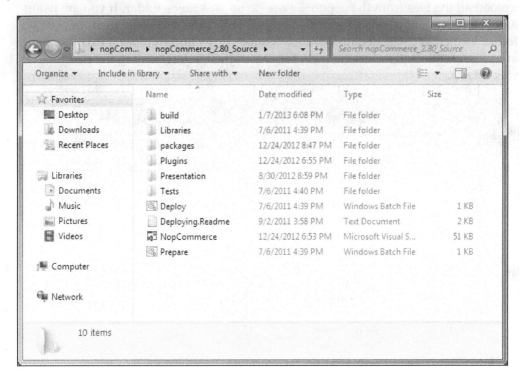

Double-click on the Deploy.bat file to start the process. This file will build the website and create a new folder called Deployable, which is located in the same location. Inside this new folder will be a folder titled nop_2.80, which will contain all the files to upload.

 Visual Studio is required to run the Deploy.bat file. Visual Studio is also needed to build and compile the source code into a deployable format.

Your hosting account should have a root folder where all your web application files will be uploaded. Using your FTP program, connect to your hosting provider and upload all the files from the Deployable/nop_2.80 folder. If you are using a development environment, simply copy all of the files and paste them to your IIS folder located at C:\inetpub\wwwroot (choose **Copy and Replace** if existing files are present; this will ensure the new files are copied in but existing file permissions stay intact).

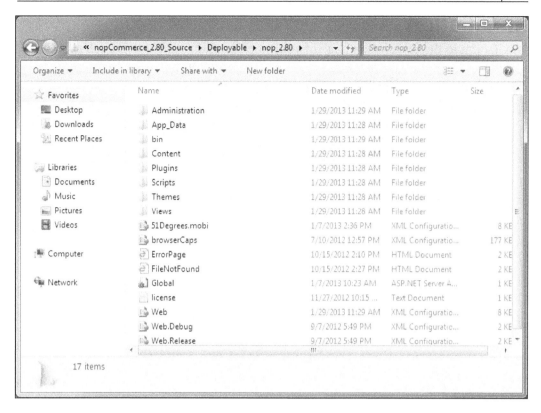

Once all the files are uploaded, open a web browser and navigate to the following URL:

`http://www.YOURDOMAINNAME.com/install`

Here, YOURDOMAINNAME is the domain name you chose and attached to your hosting account. If you are using a development environment, navigate to `http://localhost/install`.

Real world

When uploading your site to your hosting provider, there are some folders you may not want to upload. For instance, the `Content` folder holds all the product images that nopCommerce displays to users. These images are generated by the system and may be held in the `Content` folder. If you upload your local copy, you may overwrite images you don't mean to.

Installation

Navigating to the installation page of your nopCommerce site will launch the installation process. This is a guided installation, and you will need to provide some information for the install to successfully complete.

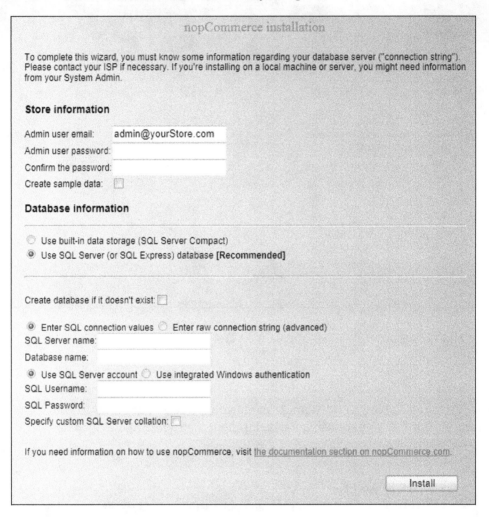

You'll need to enter the following details:

- **Admin user e-mail**: This is the e-mail address for the first admin of the site.
- **Admin password**: You will need to supply a password for the admin account.

- **Create sample data**: Check this box if you would like sample products to be created. This is recommended so you can start working with your site before adding any of your own products. You can always delete these items later, or unpublish them so they no longer appear on your site.

- **Database Information**: Here you can select either SQL Server Compact or SQL Server. It is recommended to use a full SQL Server product, not the Compact edition.

- **Create database if doesn't exist**: It is recommended that you create your database and database user beforehand to ensure a successful installation. Simply create a database instance and add the database user to it. The installation process will create all the tables, stored procedures, and so on.

- **SQL Server name**: This is the IP, URL, or server name for your database. You will get your SQL Server name from your hosting provider.

- **Database name**: This is the name of the database used by nopCommerce. If you opted to create your database ahead of time, use the name you gave your database here.

- **Use SQL Server account/Use integrated Windows authentication**: If you are installing at a hosting provider, you can use your SQL Server account and supply the credentials you created with your database. If you are using a development environment, you can select Windows authentication. If you are using Windows authentication, the account hosting the application pool in IIS must be a user in the database.

- **Specify Custom SQL Server collation**: This is an advanced setting and should be left unchecked.

After all the required information has been provided, click on **Install**. You will be presented with the installation progress screen.

Once the installation is complete, you will be presented with the homepage of your new storefront.

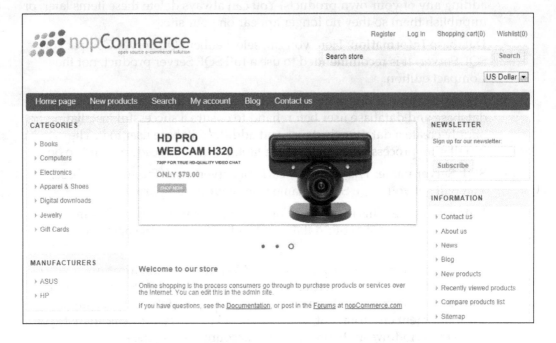

Setting up file permissions

nopCommerce requires write permissions for various files and folders. Write permissions allow nopCommerce to modify these files as you make changes to the environment. During the installation process, permissions will be validated for these items. If you do not have appropriate permissions set up, a warning message will be displayed with items that need to be configured.

The following folders and files need write permissions:

- Folders:
    - `App_Data`
    - `Bin`
    - `Content` (all child folders as well)
    - `Plugins`
    - `Plugins\Bin`

- Files:
  - ° `Global.asax`
  - ° `Web.config`

If you find that you need permissions modified, please check with your hosting provider to help you modify these folders and files. Some providers allow you to modify permissions from your hosting control panel, while others will require technical support in order to modify these for you.

If you are deploying to a development environment, this should not be an issue, as you should already have appropriate permissions.

Summary

In this chapter, you were introduced to the various download options for nopCommerce as well as its prerequisites and requirements. You also learned about how to set up your development environment if you wanted to perform any custom development. You then learned how to install nopCommerce and how to set the necessary permissions. In the next chapter, you'll explore the storefront and dig into the customer experience.

2
The Public-facing Storefront

The public-facing storefront of nopCommerce is your e-commerce store. It is the site where customers will come from the Web to learn about your company, browse your products, place items in the shopping cart, and if all goes well, buy stuff! The storefront is made up of many components. This chapter will cover the most important parts and, generally speaking, the most frequently used parts of your website. With any e-commerce site, there are certain pages and areas where customers will spend the majority of their time, namely product pages, the shopping cart, and the checkout. However, there are a lot of other pages that customers will use, and it's important that you, the store owner, are very familiar with all the pages in your site. Just as a ship captain will know every bolt and weld of their ship, you should know every page your customers may visit. Even though we may only be covering the most viewed pages in this chapter, you should plan to take the time to thoroughly navigate your site just as any customer would.

All examples in this chapter are taken from a base nopCommerce installation that used the **Create sample data** option during the install process.

General site layout and overview

When customers navigate to your store, they will be presented with the homepage. The homepage is where we'll begin to review the site layout and structure.

1. **Logo**: This is your store logo. As with just about every e-commerce site, this serves as a link back to your homepage.

2. **Header links**: The toolbar holds some of the most frequently used links, such as Shopping cart, Wishlist, and Account. These links are very customer focused, as this area will also show the customer's logged in status once they are registered with your site.

3. **Header menu**: The menu holds various links to other important pages, such as New products, Search, and Contact us. It also contains the link to the built-in blog site.

4. **Left-side menu**: The left-side menu serves as a primary navigation area. It contains the Categories and Manufacturers links as well as Tags and Polls.

5. **Center**: This area is the main content of the site. It will hold category and product information, as well as the main content of the homepage.

6. **Right-side menu**: The right-side menu holds links to other ancillary pages in your site, such as Contact us, About us, and News. It also holds the Newsletter signup widget.

7. **Footer**: The footer holds the copyright information and the **Powered by nopCommerce** license tag.

 The naming conventions used for these areas are driven by the Cascading Style Sheet (CSS) definitions. For instance, if you look at the CSS for the **Header links** area, you will see a definition of `header-links`.

nopCommerce uses layouts to define the overall site structure. A layout is a type of page used in ASP.NET MVC to define a common site template, which is then inherited across all the other pages on your site. In nopCommerce, there are several different layout pages used throughout the site. There are two main layout pages that define the core structure:

- **Root head**: This is the base layout page. It contains the header of the HTML that is generated and is responsible for loading all the CSS and JavaScript files needed for the site.

- **Root**: This layout is responsible for loading the header, footer, and contains the Master Wrapper, which contains all the other content of the page.

These two layouts are common for all pages within nopCommerce, which means every page in the site will display the logo, header links, header menu, and footer. They form the foundation of the site structure. The site pages themselves will utilize one of three other layouts that determine the structure inside the Master Wrapper:

- **Three-column**: The three-column layout is what the nopCommerce homepage utilizes. It includes the right side, left side, and center areas. This layout is used primarily on the homepage.

- **Two-column**: This is the most common layout that customers will encounter. It includes the left side and center areas. This layout is used on all category and product pages as well as all the ancillary pages.

- **One-column**: This layout is used in the shopping cart and checkout pages. It includes the center area only.

Changing the layout page used by certain pages requires changing the code. For instance, if we open the product page in Visual Studio, we can see the layout page being used:

```
NopCommerce - Microsoft Visual Studio Express 2012 for Web

FILE    EDIT    VIEW    PROJECT    BUILD    DEBUG    TEAM    TOOLS    TEST    WINDOW    HELP

ProductTemplate.SingleVariant.cshtml

@model ProductDetailsModel
@using Nop.Core.Domain.Seo;
@using Nop.Core.Infrastructure;
@using Nop.Web.Models.Catalog;
@{
    Layout = "~/Views/Shared/_ColumnsTwo.cshtml";

    //title, meta
    Html.AddTitleParts(!String.IsNullOrEmpty(Model.MetaTitle) ? Model.MetaTit
    Html.AddMetaDescriptionParts(Model.MetaDescription);
    Html.AddMetaKeywordParts(Model.MetaKeywords);
```

As you can see, the layout defined for this page is `_ColumnsTwo.cshtml`, the two-column layout. You can change the layout used by updating this property, for instance, to `_ColumnsThree.cshtml`, to use the three-column layout.

Category and manufacturer pages

When adding new products to the site, you can specify their category and manufacturer. These groupings allow customers to search for products on your site more easily.

Category pages display a collection of products that you have grouped under that category. For instance, all books are grouped under the category **Books**. A customer can navigate to any category located in the left-side area. Once a customer navigates to a particular category, that category link will become bold to indicate to the customer where they currently are. The breadcrumb will also update with the current location.

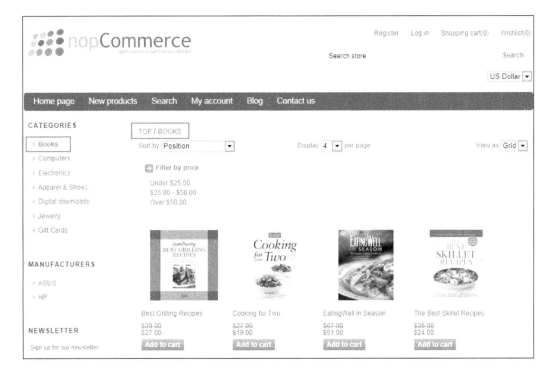

Categories may also have subcategories to further group your products. For instance, a Computers category may have subcategories that include Desktops, Laptops, and Accessories. If a category has subcategories, the customer will be presented with a page displaying the subcategories. In addition, the left-side area will expand to show the subcategories under the parent category.

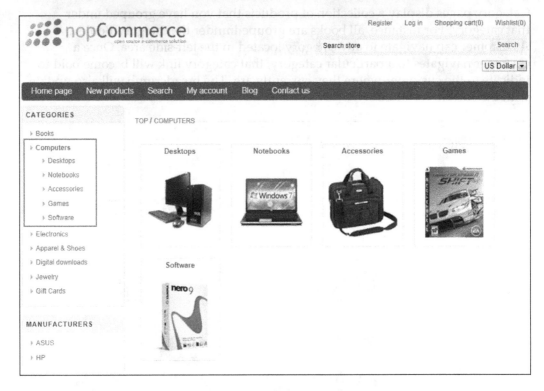

Clicking on a subcategory on this page will take the customer to a page displaying all the products for that particular subcategory. The breadcrumb will also update to reflect that the customer is in a subcategory.

Manufacturer pages behave similarly. All products grouped under a certain manufacturer can be displayed together. Customers can navigate to a manufacturer page from the left-side area. Clicking on a particular manufacturer name will display all the products for that manufacturer. As with the category pages, the link will become bold, but there is no breadcrumb on these pages. This is replaced with the manufacturer name instead.

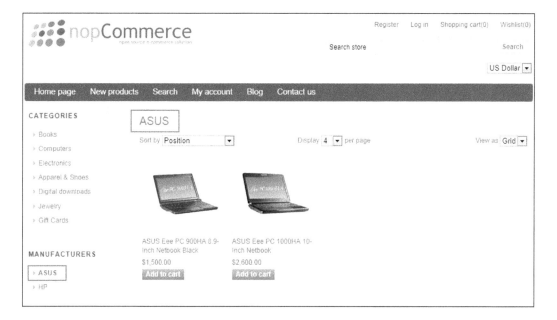

Product pages

Product pages are the heart and soul of your site. This is where the majority of a customer's time is spent. Your site will typically have more product pages than any other type of page. Because of this, product pages have a lot of components to them.

1. **Product pictures**: Product pictures make up a good portion of the product page. You can add multiple pictures to products, which show up as thumbnail images under the main picture. Clicking the thumbnail image will open a modal window allowing the customer to scroll through all the available images.

2. **Product name**: This is the name of the product and it is displayed on the product page, category pages, search results, and so on. It will be shown anywhere the product is referenced in the site.

3. **Short description**: The product short description is shown on the product page directly underneath the product name. It's meant to be a quick description of the product that gives the most important information.

4. **Display stock availability**: You have the option to display stock availability of products when tracking their inventory, by their general availability or the actual stock count. You can also choose not to show this at all, for instance, for drop ship items. These settings can be managed in the administration site.

5. **Review and rate link**: Customers can review products on your site by clicking on this link. Customers will be directed to a review page where a written review and a rating can be given. The ratings range from 1 to 5 stars. By default, all reviews must be approved by a site administrator before they will appear on the product page. This can be changed in the administration site.

6. **Price**: This is the product price. You can also define sale prices for your products. If you give a product a sale price, the old price will be shown in red with a strike through and the sale price will be displayed.

7. **Quantity**: Customers can enter the product quantity they wish to purchase using this textbox. The default value is 1. If the customer requests more quantity than is currently available, they will be notified that the quantity exceeds the on-hand count, which will be displayed to them.

8. **Add to cart**: Clicking on this button will add the product to the customer's shopping cart. Once customers click on the **Add to Cart** button, they will be presented with a spinning wheel notification, after which they are notified if the item was successfully added to their cart via the notification bar that appears at the top of the product page.

9. **Add to wishlist**: Customers can add products to their wishlist by clicking on this button. The wishlist is simply a set of items the customer would like to keep track of but not purchased right away. Once products are placed in the wishlist, a customer can navigate to the Wishlist page by clicking the link in the Header Links area at the top of the page. The Wishlist page also includes the **Email a friend** functionality, as well as a public URL you can share with friends.

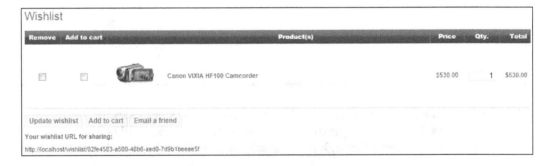

10. **Email a Friend**: Customers can e-mail a friend a link to any product on your site. Clicking on this button will direct customers to the **Email a friend** page where they can provide an e-mail address for their friend as well as a personal message. By default, only registered customers are allowed to use this feature. This can be changed in the administration site.

11. **Add to compare list**: Clicking on this button will add the current product to the **Compare products** list and will then direct customers to that page. This allows customers to compare various attributes of products on a single page. To compare multiple products, customers must navigate to each product page and click on the **Add to compare list** button. Customers can also navigate directly to the **Compare products** page from the homepage by clicking on the **Compare product list** link in the information area.

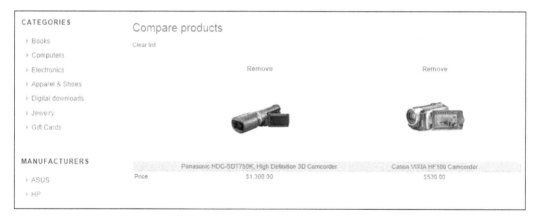

12. **Add this**: This area allows customers to share the product page with customers via social media channels, such as Facebook, Twitter, and LinkedIn. This is powered by the **Add this** widget (`http://www.addthis.com`). This widget can be modified in the administration site, as well as replaced with other social media widgets from other companies.

13. **Full description**: This is the full and complete product description. This description is generally longer and much more detailed. This area supports full HTML when editing in the administration site so that you can include styling such as bulleted lists using a WYSIWYG editor.

14. **Product tags**: Each product can have tags associated with it. These tags show up on each product as well as in the Popular Tags area on the homepage. It's a way to further group certain products together based on their tags. For instance, you could group laptops together based on whether they offer a backlit keyboard. This feature is not enough to warrant a category or subcategory, but may be important to your customers. This way they could click on a **backlit keyboard** tag to see all the products that have been tagged with this word.

15. **Related products**: Related products could be considered as cross sells. However, do not confuse the two. Related products are specific products that you want to show with a particular product. You can add and edit these by product in the administration site. You can also add cross sells, but these products will show up in the shopping cart rather than on the product page.

> The naming conventions used for these areas are driven by how these areas are defined in the administration site. For instance, when adding or editing a product, you will see the same naming conventions used, such as Short Description, Full Description, and so on.

Searching for products

Customers can search your site in two ways—by either clicking the **Search** link in the header menu or by using the search textbox under the Header Links area.

The **Search** textbox features an auto-complete function, which will show up the product names that match with what the customer is typing. For instance, if we type canon into the search box, a list of product names that match canon will be shown in the drop-down list.

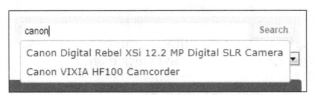

Clicking on any of the results in the drop-down list will take you directly to the product page. Alternatively, the customer can click the **Search** button and will be directed to a search results page that will display more information about each product.

On the search results page, there is an **Advanced Search** checkbox. By clicking on this, the customer will be presented with further options to refine their search, such as Category, Manufacturer, Price Range, as well as the ability to search product descriptions in addition to the product names.

Shopping cart

When a customer clicks on the **Add to cart** button on the product page, the site will add that product in the quantity selected to the shopping cart. nopCommerce technically has two shopping carts, namely the mini shopping cart and the shopping cart.

The mini shopping cart is visible when a customer hovers over the **Shopping cart** link located in the Header Links area. It shows the customer items that are currently in the shopping cart, as well as the sub-total cost for those items. You can configure how many items to display in the mini shopping cart in the administration site. From the mini shopping cart, the customer can go to the shopping cart page or begin the checkout process.

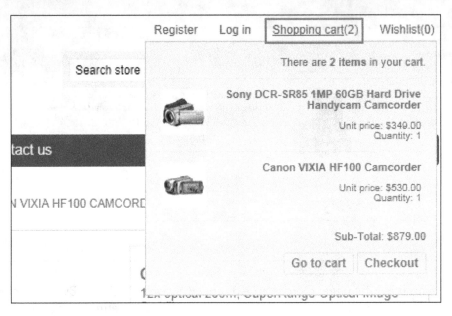

The shopping cart on the other hand is a full page that basically kicks off the checkout process. As you'll see, it has quite a few more features than the mini shopping cart.

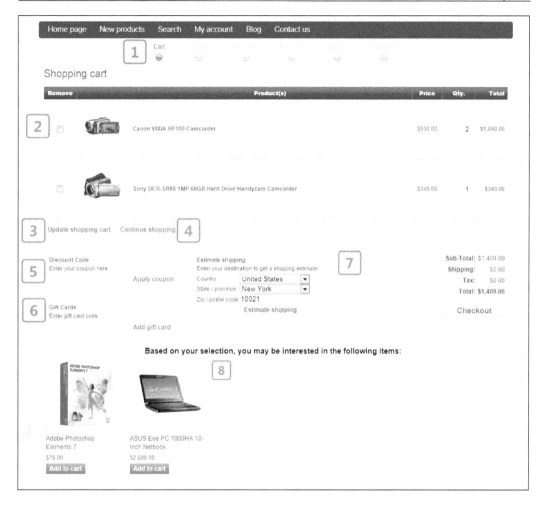

1. **Checkout progress**: This progress bar indicates to the customer where they are in the checkout process.

2. **Cart items**: All the items in the shopping cart will be listed in this area along with the quantity placed in the cart, the product price, and a total for each line item. Customers can remove items from the cart by checking the checkbox next to the item and clicking on the **Update shopping cart** button. Customers can also update the quantities in the same way, by changing the number in the **Qty** textbox.

3. **Update shopping cart**: Clicking on this button will update the shopping cart with any changes entered in the **Cart items** area.

4. **Continue shopping**: Clicking on this button will direct customers back to the homepage of your site.

5. **Discount Code**: This is where customers can enter a coupon or discount codes that you have set up for your store.

6. **Gift Cards**: Gift cards can be redeemed in this area.

7. **Estimate Shipping**: Customers can get estimated shipping rates using this area. By default, this option is enabled, but this widget may not always show in the shopping cart. For instance, if you choose Fixed Rate shipping, the **Estimate Shipping** area will not display.

8. **Cross sells**: Individual products can have cross sells attached to them. If a product in the shopping cart has cross-sell products attached, they will be displayed here.

Checkout and order details

By default, nopCommerce utilizes a one-page checkout process. Basically, this means the customer will not leave the page during checkout, and the various sections of the checkout page will update as the customer completes them. This is a more modern checkout process, and nopCommerce handles it well.

The Billing Address and Shipping Address sections in these examples show a drop-down list with addresses pre-filled. This is because this checkout is taking place with a registered customer who is logged in to the site. If no addresses exist for the current customer checking out, then the appropriate form fields will be displayed to capture address information.

If you prefer, you can change this in the administration site, and instead make the site use an individual page for each checkout step. However, this book will only cover the one page checkout process.

The checkout process is split into the following six sections:

- **Billing Address**: This is the billing address for the customer. This is typically the billing address for a credit card if one is being used during checkout.

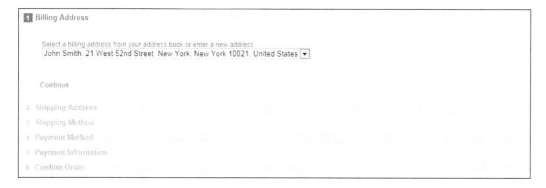

- **Shipping Address**: This is the delivery address for the customer.

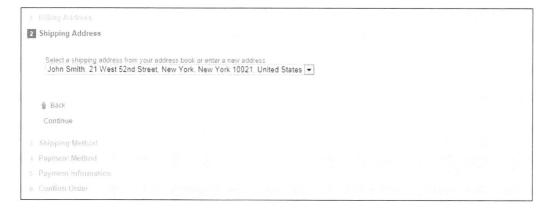

- **Shipping Method**: Here customers can select the shipping method they wish to use. These methods are configurable in the administration site, including the methods you wish to offer and how much you wish to charge.

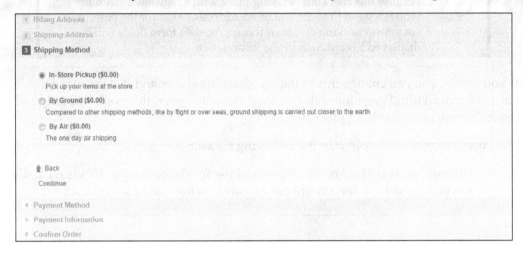

- **Payment Method**: Customers can select their preferred payment method in this step. By default, several payment options are available, but these are configurable in the administration site. In most cases, your site will offer credit card as the only payment option.

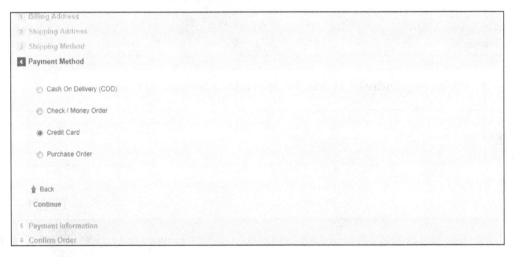

- **Payment Information**: This section is where your customer will enter their payment information. This section will change based on which payment method the customer chose. For instance, credit card fields will be displayed for a credit card payment method, whereas Purchase Order will show a textbox to capture a single PO number.

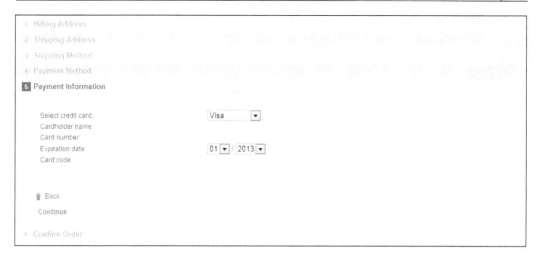

- **Confirm Order**: This section will display all the order details to the customer, including displaying the items they are ordering, shipping and billing information, and totals. At the bottom of this section is the **Confirm** button. The order is processed after the customer clicks on the **Confirm** button.

- **Order Details**: Once the customer confirms the order, it is processed by the site and the order details page is displayed.

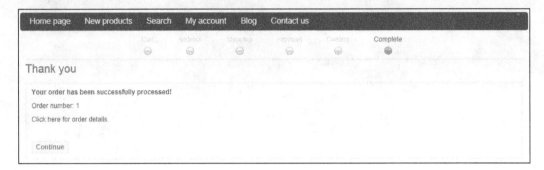

- **Order information**: This is a very basic page that displays a confirmation to the customer that the order was successfully processed. It also displays a link to view the order details, where the customer can also print a copy of their receipt. An e-mail receipt is also generated at this point and mailed to the customer.

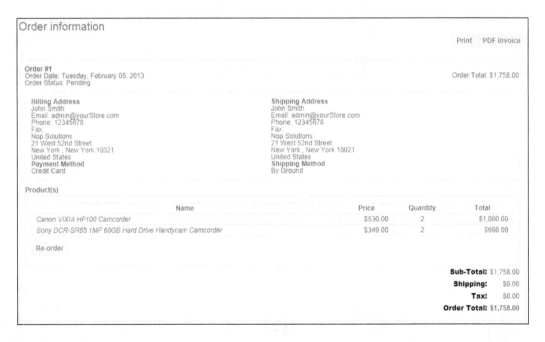

When beginning the checkout process, the customer has the option to create an account or check out as a guest. If they create an account, customers can view all their past orders by logging in to your store.

Summary

In this chapter, you took a deep dive into the storefront and the customer experience. You got an overview of the general store layouts and how they are used throughout the site. You learned about category and manufacturer pages and got an in-depth view of the product pages. You also saw how customers will search for products on your site, as well as how they can add them to the shopping cart. Finally, you learned how the one-page checkout process works in nopCommerce and saw the order confirmation details your customers will receive.

In the next chapter you'll learn about the administration site, where you'll configure your store and set up products.

3
The Administration Site

The administration site is where you, the storeowner, will spend the majority of your time. Just about every aspect of your store can be managed from this site. This is where you will create and manage your products, process orders, and update settings throughout the store. There are hundreds of settings in the administration site, and at first it can seem a little overwhelming. As with the public-facing storefront, you should take the time to educate yourself and investigate everything in the administration site. This chapter will cover some of the more important areas of the site, mostly those related to selling products!

 All examples in this chapter are taken from a base nopCommerce installation that used the **Create sample data** option during the installation process. This can be an invaluable tool for experimenting with your site, as the sample products demonstrate many different product types and configurations. I always recommend using this feature as these sample products can easily be deleted after you have created your site.

How to access and overview

Accessing the administration site is something that only administrators can do. When you install nopCommerce, you are required to create the first administrator account. By default, this account is admin@yourstore.com, which is prefilled when you run the installation process. However, no matter which account you set up during installation, there will be a single administrator account when you are done.

You can add as many administrator accounts as you like; however, it's best practice to keep the number of administrators small to help control your site. Once someone is added to the administrator list, they can access the administration site by simply logging in to the site. Once you are logged in, if you are an administrator, you will be having a link at the very top of the screen titled **Administration**, as shown here:

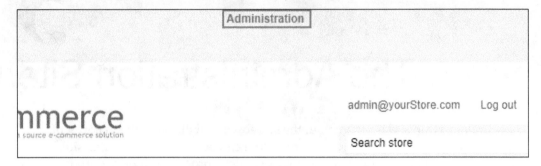

Clicking this link will take you to the administration site and the homepage. Let's review the components of the administration site:

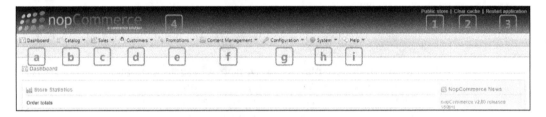

- **Public store (1)**: Clicking this link will simply open the public storefront.

- **Clear cache (2)**: When nopCommerce launches for the first time, it will cache a lot of content from the database to increase site performance. A cache stores recently-used information in a place where it can be accessed extremely quickly, without accessing the database each time. There are some settings that you can change in the administration site that are cached. If you make a change and it does not appear immediately, then you may need to clear the cache. Clicking this link will clear the cache for the site.

- **Restart application (3)**: Clicking this link will restart nopCommerce. It will clear the cache and recycle the application pool in IIS. There may be instances where new code is deployed, perhaps a plugin, after which you may be required to restart the application. Please note, this will interrupt the service of the site and customers may experience some downtime during this operation, usually lasting only a few minutes.

- **The menu bar (4)**: The menu in the administration site gives you access to all of the areas needed to manage the site:

    ○ **Dashboard (a)**: This is a link back to the dashboard home page in the administration site.

    ○ **Catalog (b)**: This area allows you to manage categories, manufacturers, products, and product attributes. This is where you will essentially define the structure of your site with categories and where you'll load new products for sale on the site.

    ○ **Sales (c)**: The **Sales** area allows you to manage orders, shipping, gift cards, current shopping carts, and more. Once orders are placed, this is where you will go to process and ship them.

    ○ **Customers (d)**: You can manage your customers via this area. This includes adding and reporting customers, as well as maintaining your administrator list.

    ○ **Promotions (e)**: Under **Promotions** you can manage your site's discounts, affiliates, and newsletter subscriptions. Site discounts include promotion codes as well as global discounts that do not require codes.

    ○ **Content Management (f)**: This area is where you can manage the built-in blog and forums, as well as the topics (pages) and message templates. The two main areas here are topics and message templates. Topics are the ancillary pages on your site such as **About Us** or **Contact Us**. Message templates are the outbound e-mails that are generated by the site.

    ○ **Configuration (g)**: This is quite a large area, and will be covered in more detail in *Chapter 4, Configuring the Store*. This area allows you to configure most aspects of your site, including the store name, URL, themes, payment methods, shipping methods, tax settings, and so on. These settings make up the bulk of configuring your site. You should plan to spend a lot of time exploring this area to learn all about your available configuration options.

    ○ **System (h)**: This area holds information about the site, the server hosting the site, logs, scheduled tasks, and the message queue. The log is an important area to keep your eye on because it will display any site errors as they occur.

    ○ **Help (i)**: This menu option contains links back to the nopCommerce site, including a link to the forums where you can ask questions to other nopCommerce users.

The home page of the administration site is the dashboard. This page displays the current store statistics, including a summary of orders, registered customers, and best-selling products. The dashboard, shown in the following screenshot, is a page you'll look forward to viewing each day as your site grows:

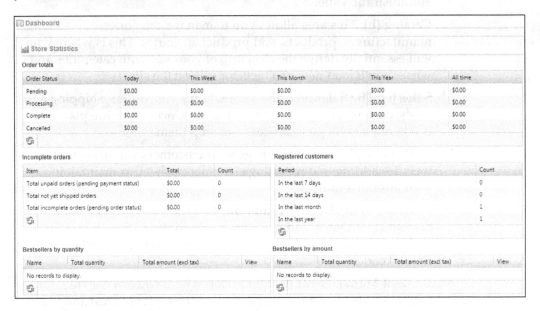

Follow along to know more about the dashboard:

- **Order totals**: This grid is a summary of all the orders customers have placed on your site. It includes numbers from the current day, the current week, the current month, the current year, and all time. It also breaks the orders out by their status, including **Pending**, **Processing**, **Complete**, and **Cancelled**. Depending on how you have your site configured, you may not have data for some of these statuses. For instance, if you are processing orders using credit cards and have the payment method set up to authorize and capture at the same time, you would only have data in the **Complete** and **Cancelled** statuses.

- **Incomplete orders**: This grid shows all the orders that are incomplete. This may include unpaid, not yet shipped, or incomplete orders. As with **Order totals**, the data that is displayed here will be determined by how your site is configured.

- **Registered customers**: This grid shows the count of all the customers who have registered on your site. This includes counts for the last 7 days, the last 14 days, the last month, and the last year. In your initial installation, you will see a single user that has registered; this is the base administrator account. These numbers will only be for registered customers, so if you have **Anonymous Checkout** enabled, those customers will not show up in these counts.

- **Bestsellers by quantity**: This grid will list the products that are your bestsellers by how many units you've sold.

- **Bestsellers by amount**: This grid will list the products that are your bestsellers by the total amount of dollars.

As you can see, the dashboard has a lot of great information that provides a quick overview of how your store is performing.

Creating and managing categories

Before you create any products, you'll want to create some categories for those products to be grouped under. To view your current categories, you can navigate to the **Categories** section from the menu bar (**Catalog | Categories | List or Catalog | Categories | Tree View**).

There are two options available to view your current categories:

- **List**: This view will display all the categories you have set up as well as all the subcategories in the default view. This grid also displays whether the category is published and its display order. You can edit any category in the list by clicking on the **Edit** link, as shown in the following screenshot:

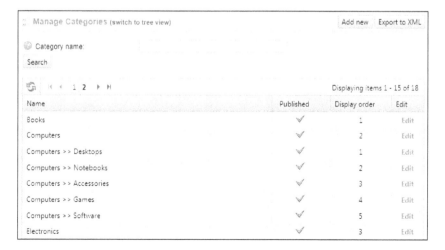

Name	Published	Display order	Edit
Books	✓	1	Edit
Computers	✓	2	Edit
Computers >> Desktops	✓	1	Edit
Computers >> Notebooks	✓	2	Edit
Computers >> Accessories	✓	3	Edit
Computers >> Games	✓	4	Edit
Computers >> Software	✓	5	Edit
Electronics	✓	3	Edit

Displaying items 1 - 15 of 18

- **Tree View**: This gives you a hierarchal look at your current categories. Each main category is listed, and if subcategories are present, an arrow icon is shown. Clicking on the arrow will expand the list and show the subcategories. This can be a helpful view if you are building out new categories that are not yet published, as it will it show you how the navigation on the site will be laid out. Clicking on any of the categories will bring up the edit screen.

To create new categories, simply click on the **Add New** button, which is located on either view in the upper-right corner of the screen. This will bring you to the **Add a New Category** page:

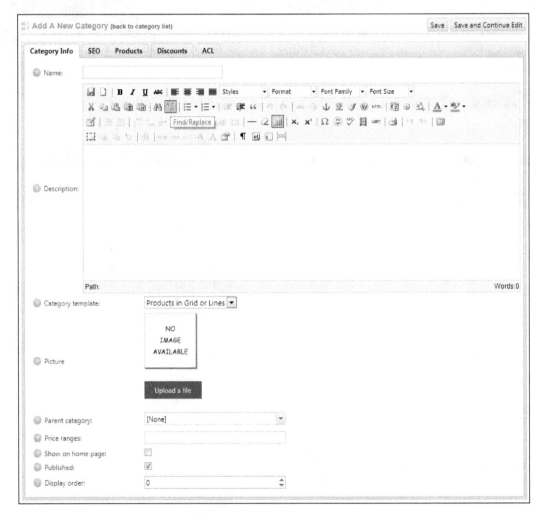

Here is a detailed explanation of this page:

- **Name**: The category name will appear in the navigation as well as in other places throughout the site. It should be short and descriptive of the category.

- **Description**: This is a full description of the category and can include HTML content. This content will be shown at the top of the category page before any products. If you do not wish to show any content here, you can leave the description blank.

- **Category template**: The base installation of nopCommerce only includes one category template. But if you install or develop more templates, you can choose them here.

- **Picture**: This is a picture for the category. If this category is marked as **Show on home page**, this image will be used. When you have subcategories, navigating to the main or parent category will display a page with all the subcategories listed along with the image that is uploaded here. For instance, in the following screenshot, the **Computers** category will display images for all the subcategories grouped within it:

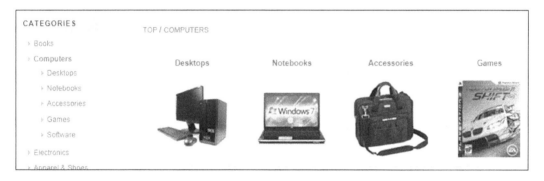

- **Parent category**: If the category you are creating is a subcategory, you can select the parent category here.

- **Price ranges**: To show a price range filter on the category page, you can supply values here. Values must be separated by semicolons and must include a dash to specify the range. A dash with no value in front of it produces an **Under** option, and a dash with no value after it produces an **Over** option. For instance, **-25;25-50;50-;** will produce the options shown in the following screenshot:

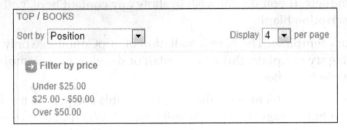

- **Show on home page**: Checking this box will make the category appear on the home page. The category picture will be used as a link to the category.

- **Published**: **Published** indicates if this category should appear on the site. If this is checked, the category will appear in the navigation. You can uncheck this to effectively hide it from customers. This can be useful when creating new categories or if you have seasonal categories that should not appear all year long.

- **Display order**: This is the order in which the categories will appear in the navigation.

There are also other tabs on this page that allow you to control other aspects of the category:

- **SEO**: You can specify metadata information for the category page, which is used by search engines. You can also set the page size for the category pages here.

- **Products**: From here you can manage which products appear under a certain category. You can also place products into categories from the product administration screens, but this tab will display a grid of all the products currently grouped under the category.

- **Discounts**: If you have discounts set up that apply to categories, you can map them here. Before any discounts show up in this tab, they first must be created and scoped to apply to categories.

- **ACL**: The **Access Control List** (ACL) allows you to specify if this category should display to everyone who visits the site, or instead just to specific groups. For instance, you could specify a category-only display for administrators, effectively hiding it from other customers on your site.

Creating and managing manufacturers

You can also group products by manufacturers, allowing your customers to view all the products by certain brands. To view your current manufacturers, you can navigate to **Catalog | Manufacturers** from the menu bar:

This grid will display all the current manufacturers. The grid also displays whether the manufacturer is published and its display order. You can edit any category in the list by clicking on the **Edit** link.

To add a new manufacturer, click on the **Add New** button at the top-right corner of the page. This will bring up the **Add a New Manufacturer** page.

The layout of the manufacturer's page is identical to the **Category** page. All the same options appear and you will manage manufacturers in the exact same way. The only difference between these two is how they are displayed to the customer on the storefront.

Creating and managing products

Managing your products is a big part of running your storefront. Products have a lot of properties to configure and how you set them up will depend on a number of things. Before we begin, we need to explore the concept of product variants.

Every product you set up to sell will have at least one product variant. You can think of these in the terms of parent and child relationships. Each product will have a number of base properties that are needed to list the item for sale. These include things such as name, description, category, manufacturer, and so on. Product variants are different variations of the base product that include more detailed properties such as images, cost, price, and so on.

The easiest way to think about products and product variants is with an example. Let's say you have a t-shirt you want to sell. The t-shirt comes in many different colors, and perhaps some of those colors cost more to manufacture. In this scenario, you can set up a base t-shirt product with properties that are the same for all the t-shirts regardless of the color. Then you would create a product variant for each t-shirt color under the parent item. On the site, the customer would see the base parent product and underneath would be the product variants to choose from.

You do not have to have multiple product variants. If you are creating a product with no variants, it will still have one variant. This is called a single product variant, as all products must have at least one product and one product variant. Looking back at the t-shirt example, you could be selling band t-shirts, in which case you would only need one product variant as the logo and colors would be different for each shirt.

You have several options to help you manage your products. To view these options, you can navigate to the category's section from **Catalog | Products**. Under the products' fly-out menu, you have the following options:

- **Manage Products**: This page will display all the products you have set up on your site. You can filter these by category, manufacturer, product name, and so on. Clicking on the **Edit** link takes you to the edit product page.

- **Bulk Edit Product Variants**: You can perform bulk edits on your product variants from this page. All your product variants are listed in the grid and you can click into the grid to make edits.

- **Product Reviews**: This page will display all the product reviews that have been submitted via your product pages. From here you can approve, edit, or disapprove any reviews you had previously approved.

- **Product Tags**: This page will display a grid of all the current product tags that are available to tag with. It will also display the number of products that are currently tagged with each tag and allow you to edit the tag or delete it.

- **Low Stock Report**: If you are tracking inventory on your products, this grid will list any items that have reached a zero stock quantity. You can also configure the product to e-mail the site administrator if stock gets below a certain amount.

To add new products, navigate to **Catalog | Products | Manage Products**. On the **Manage Products** page, click on the **Add New** button. This will bring you to the **Add a New Product** page:

Read on to learn more about the different tabs in this page:

- **Product name**: This is the product name and will display whenever the product is shown, such as product page, category page, search results, shopping cart, and so on.

- **Short description**: The product short description is shown on the product page directly underneath the product name. It's meant to be a quick description of the product that gives the most important information. The short description is also sent as part of the **Email a Friend** message.

- **Full description**: This is the full and complete product description. This description is generally longer and much more detailed. This area supports full HTML when editing in the administration site, so you can include styling, such as bulleted lists, using the WYSIWYG editor.

- **Admin comment**: This is simply a comment you may want to attach to this product. It will not be displayed to the customer and is for internal use only.

- **Product template**: These are the following two options for the product template:

    ○ **Variants in Grid**: If your product has multiple variants, this template should be selected. Variants will display under the product's full description in a list, and this is where customers will add the product to their cart.

    ○ **Single Product Variant**: If you only have a single variant, this template will display an **Add to Cart** button and no other variants will be displayed.

- **Show on home page**: Check this box to have this product displayed on the home page of the site.

- **Published**: **Published** indicates if this product should appear on the site. You can uncheck this to effectively hide it from customers. This should be unchecked when creating new products until you have all your product information loaded and it is ready to sell.

- **Allow customer reviews**: You can decide to allow customer reviews at the product level. Check this box if you want to allow reviews to be submitted for this product.

- **Product tags**: Each product can have tags associated with it. These tags show up on each product as well as in the **Popular Tags** area on the home page. It's a way to further group certain products together based on their tags. For instance, you could group laptops together based on whether they offer a backlit keyboard. This feature is not enough to warrant a category or subcategory, but may be important to your customers. This way, they could click a **backlit keyboard** tag to see all the products that have been tagged with this word.

There are also other tabs on this page that allow you to control other aspects of the product:

- **SEO**: You can specify metadata information for the product page, which is used by search engines. The most important property here is **Search Engine Friendly Page Name**. With this property you can control how your product page URL is crafted. So, rather than a cryptic URL with `pid=123`, where PID is the product number, you can craft human-readable URLs with product information in them. This also helps with search engine results, as the URL has relevant information in it.

- **Default product variant info**: When you create a new product, you are required to create the first default product variant for this new product. This first product variant will need more setup after you create the product, but the majority of the information can be supplied here. This will be discussed in further detail shortly.

- **Category mappings**: You can map this product to one or many categories in this tab.

- **Manufacturer mappings**: You can map this product to one or many manufacturers in this tab, although it will most likely only have one manufacturer.

- **Related products**: You can assign related products to this product here. These related items will display on the product page under the **Related Products** heading.

- **Cross sells**: Cross sells appear in the shopping cart under the **Based on your selection, you may be interested in the following items** heading. Choose these items carefully, as you do not want to clutter the shopping cart with a lot of extra items.

- **Pictures**: You can add multiple images to each product. This tab allows you to manage all the images you have uploaded for this product, including the order in which they appear.

- **Specification attributes**: You can set up and use product specification attributes for products. These are usually property descriptions about the product, for example: CPU type, memory size, hard drive capacity, and so on. If you apply these to a product, they will display as a grid under the full description on the product page.

- **ACL**: This tab allows you to specify if this product should display to everyone who visits the site or just to specific groups. For instance, you could specify a product-only display for administrators, effectively hiding it from other customers on your site.

 The majority of the settings under the tabs cannot be used until you save the product for the first time. This is because the product must be created before you can assign additional properties to it, such as category and manufacturer. You can click on the **Save and Continue Edit** button at any time to save the product and keep working on it.

When creating a new product, don't worry too much about filling out the default product variant. After you save the product, the **Default product variant info** tab becomes the **Product variants** tab. Under this tab is a grid that lists all your variants. You can edit any variant here or add new ones. You also get more properties after you have a default variant saved.

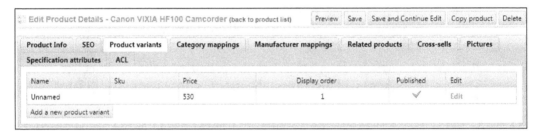

Clicking on the **Edit** link in the grid will bring up the **Edit Product Variant For Product** page. If you would like to add a new variant, simply click on the **Add a New Product Variant** button.

The **Add New/Edit Product Variant For Product** page is quite large and has many components. Let's take a look at this page in parts to make it easier to cover.

 Other properties may appear here depending on your product setup. The most common properties are covered in this chapter.

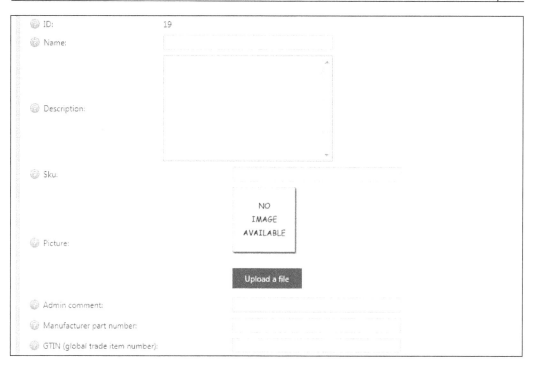

- **ID**: This is the system-generated variant ID.

- **Name**: This is the name of the variant. If you are using single product variants, you do not need to fill this out. It's more important when you have multiple variants. Single product variants will use the parent product name.

- **Description**: This is the description of the variant.

- **Sku**: The SKU is an internal tracking number for this product. If you require SKUs for your product management, input it here.

- **Picture**: You can upload a picture that is unique to this variant. The parent product will have its own pictures, and you can use this picture to show differences in the variant. It will display in the variant grid if the product has multiple variants.

- **Admin comment**: This is simply a comment you may want to attach to this product. It will not be displayed to the customer and is for internal use only.

- **Manufacturer part number**: If this product has a manufacturer part number, you can input it here.

- **GITN**: This is where you would input a UPC, ISBN, EAN, JAN, and so on.

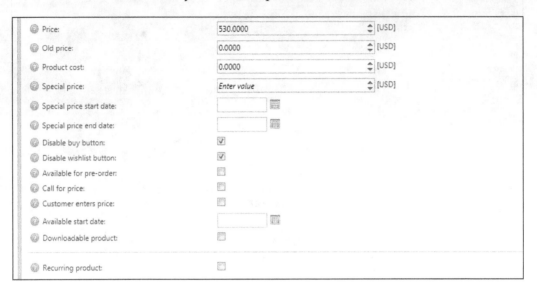

- **Price**: This is the retail price of the product.
- **Old price**: Using the **Old price** property, you can put products on sale. You can enter the sale price into the **Price** textbox and the original price into the **Old Price** textbox. This will cause the site to render the old price with a strikethrough and the price in red.
- **Product cost**: This is your cost to purchase the product. It is for internal use only and is not shown to the customer.
- **Special price**: You can enter special prices for products. This is different from a sale price as it's not rendered in red along with the original price. It will render as a normal price, but you can attach dates to it and allow the site to manage the pricing displayed.
- **Special price start date** and **Special price end date**: This is the start and end date during which your special price should be displayed.
- **Disable buy button**: You may wish to list products but not allow them to be purchased via the site. You can check this box to show a product but not show an **Add to Cart** button.
- **Available for pre-order**: If you wish to sell items before you have them in stock to ship, you can check this box. It will render the **Add to Cart** button as a **Pre-Order** button instead.
- **Call for price**: You can check this box to show **Call for price** instead of an actual retail price.

- **Customer enters price**: You may allow customers to enter prices on products. This is useful for donations or other items where you do not need to control the price collected for items.

- **Available start date** and **Available end date**: You can manage when products display on your site by giving them available start and end dates.

- **Downloadable product**: If the product is not a physical item, but can be downloaded, you can check this box. Customers can download their item from their order details screen.

- **Recurring product**: Check this box if the product is a recurring item. A recurring product is one that will generate automatic orders on a set period of time, such as a book of the month or diabetic test strips. Checking this box opens options to define the recurring cycle, which can be days, weeks, months, or years. The site will use the payment method used on the first order to create a new order at each cycle.

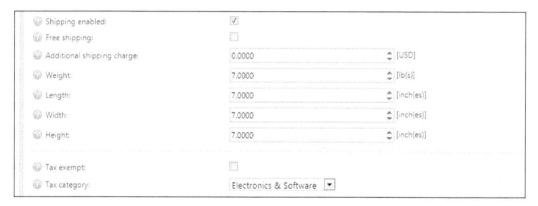

- **Shipping enabled** and **Free shipping**: You can specify if the product requires shipping. For instance, downloadable products would not need any shipping. You can also specify if this product has free shipping attached.

- **Additional shipping charge**: If this product requires additional shipping charges, enter them here. This is useful for large or heavy items.

- **Weight**, **Length**, **Width**, and **Height**: When using shipping estimations based on product dimensions, these measurements will need to be entered.

- **Tax exempt** and **Tax category**: You can manage tax classifications on your site. You can specify if this product should be subject to taxes and what tax category should apply.

You have several options when it comes to managing inventory on your site: **Don't track inventory**, **Track inventory**, and **Track inventory by product attributes**. You select which method you would like to use from the **Manage inventory method** drop-down list. The first and last methods have the same settings on this tab. The **Track inventory by product attributes** method uses **Product Attributes** to manage the inventory. **Product Attributes** is covered later in this chapter.

- **Minimum cart quantity** and **Maximum cart quantity**: You can specify the minimum and maximum quantity a customer can enter for each product. By default, these are **1** and **10,000**.

- **Allowed quantities**: By default, the product page displays a textbox allowing the customer to enter the quantity they wish to purchase. Entering values here will display a drop-down list of values instead. The values here should be comma separated, that is, **1,2,3,4,5**.

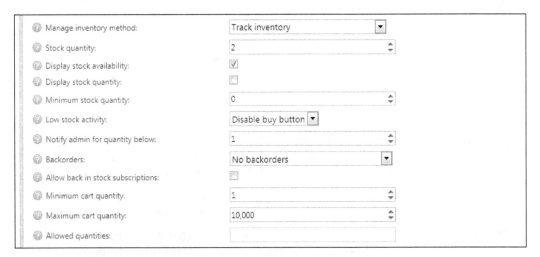

- **Stock quantity**: This is the quantity you have in stock for this variant.

- **Display stock availability** and **Display stock quantity**: **Display stock availability** will show an **In/Out of stock** message on the product page. **Display stock quantity** will display the number of units from the stock quantity on the product page.

- **Minimum stock quantity**: This allows you to trigger various actions once the stock quantity reaches this number.

- **Low stock activity**: This drop-down allows you to specify what the site will do with a product that reaches the **Minimum stock quantity** number. The options are: **Nothing, Disable buy button**, and **Unpublish**.

- **Notify admin for quantity below**: You can set a number here at which point if the inventory for the variant falls below it, the administrator for the site will be notified via e-mail.

- **Backorders** and **Allow back in stock subscriptions**: You can set how the site will treat backorder scenarios. The available options are: **No backorders, Allow qty below 0**, and **Allow qty below 0 and notify customer**. If you choose **No backorders**, you can opt to allow customers to sign up for notifications for when a product is back in stock.

- **Published**: You can check this to unpublish the variant, effectively hiding it from customers on the site. This is useful if you need more time to update your variant.

- **Display order**: This is the display order of the variants.

There are also other tabs on this page that allow you to control other aspects of the product variant:

- **Tier prices**: You can opt to give discounts based on the quantity a customer purchases of an item. For instance, you can specify that an item that is $10 may only be $9 if the customer purchases 5 or more. Under this tab you can set up the tier pricing for the variant.

- **Product variant attributes**: Product variant attributes let you specify things such as color, size, and so on. You can track inventory by these attributes as well as specify if a customer needs to select an attribute before the item can be added to the cart.

- **Discounts**: If you have discounts set up that apply to products, you can attach them to the variant under this tab.

Creating and managing attributes

nopCommerce has three types of attributes that you can utilize to help the customer experience on your site. You can navigate to these via the menu bar at **Catalog | Attributes**. These include:

- **Product Attributes**: These attributes are descriptive of the product you are selling. For instance, they could include color, size, and so on. Once you create new product attributes, they can be attached to the variants of your products and also used for inventory tracking.

- **Specification Attributes**: These attributes are used purely for informational purposes. When attached to a product, they are displayed on the product page under the full description. They can also be used as filters on the category pages.

- **Checkout Attributes**: Checkout attributes are displayed in the shopping cart and give you, the storeowner, options to offer more services to your customers before they checkout. These could include offering gift wrapping or ensuring a customer has reviewed your terms of use before placing their order.

As you can see, attributes are very powerful tools to help maximize your site.

To create new product attributes, navigate to **Catalog | Attributes | Product Attributes**. In our base installation we already have some attributes present. The grid displayed shows all the current product attributes you have set up:

Product Attributes	Add new
Name	Edit
Color	Edit
Custom Text	Edit
HDD	Edit
OS	Edit
Processor	Edit
RAM	Edit
Size	Edit
Software	Edit

When adding or editing a product attribute, you only have two properties to update: **Name** and **Description**. There aren't many properties here since the values used here are product specific. So if you wanted to use **Size** as a product attribute on a variant, you would edit your product variant, and under the **Product variant attributes** tab, you would add the **Size** product attribute to the variant.

Clicking on the **View/Edit value** link on this grid row opens a new window with all the combinations that will be presented to the customer when viewing this product:

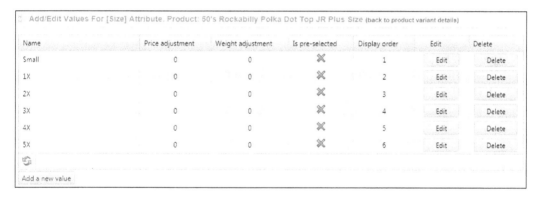

You can also specify a price adjustment for each value. For instance, if you are selling clothing that comes in XXXL, which costs you more, you can add an up-charge to the customer for those more expensive sizes.

If you have selected the **Track inventory by product attributes** inventory method for your product, you can now enter the inventory you have for each attribute value. For instance, if you are using **Size**, you can enter the inventory numbers you have for each size value. These combinations can be added under the **Product variant attributes** tab in the **Attribute combinations** tab.

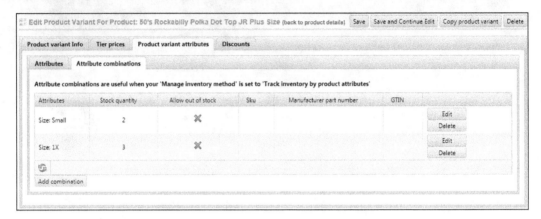

Clicking on the **Add Combination** button brings up a new window where you can add the inventory for each size value.

To create new specification attributes, navigate to **Catalog | Attributes | Specification Attributes**. The grid displayed will show all your current specification attributes:

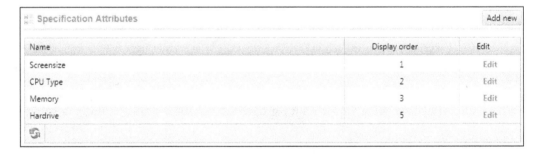

When adding or editing a specification attribute, you have more properties than a product attribute. This is because the values of a specification attribute are held on the attribute, not on the product. There are two tabs on the **Add New/Edit** page: **Attribute info** and **Options**.

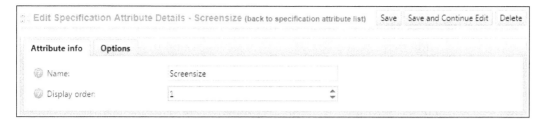

Under the **Options** tab, you can enter all the specifications for this attribute:

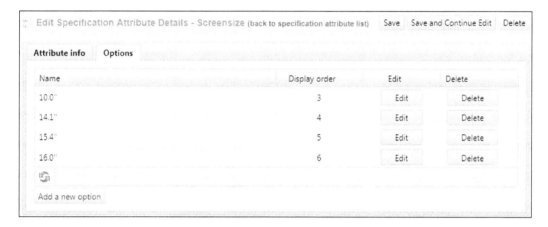

When you are adding or editing a product, you can add specifications under the **Specifications attributes** tab:

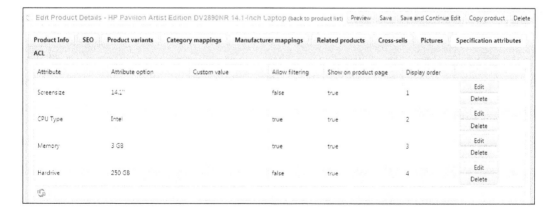

Once added to a product, specification attributes are displayed on the product page under the full description.

To create new checkout attributes, navigate to **Catalog | Attributes | Checkout Attributes**. The grid displayed will show all your current specification attributes. In the base installation there are no checkout attributes present. In this example, I have created two attributes called **Read License Agreement** and **Super Express Packing**. The former is a simple checkbox that is required and is used to ensure the customer has read a license agreement that theoretically exists on the site. The latter allows the customer to opt in for expedited packing for same day shipping. This option includes an up-charge for the service.

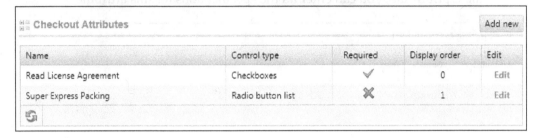

Clicking on the **Edit** link on the grid will display the attribute options:

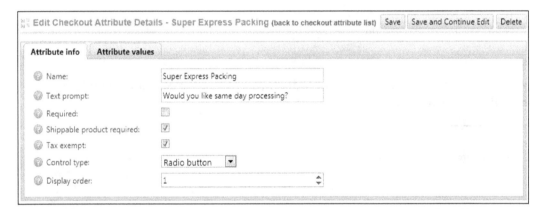

The **Text Prompt** option will be displayed to the customer in the shopping cart. You can choose the control type that the attribute will use, in this case a radio button. Under the **Attribute values** tab, you can specify the options to show the customer:

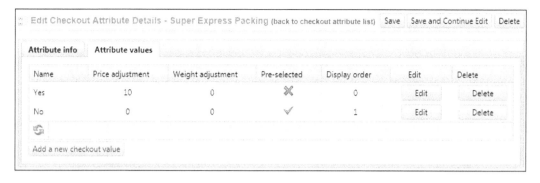

In the preceding example, we have a **Yes** and **No** option. If the customer chooses same day processing by checking **Yes**, then they will be charged an extra $10 as per the price adjustment setting.

The checkout attributes will be displayed directly under the shopping cart line items grid.

You can have as many attributes display here as you like, but take care not to overwhelm your customers here with too many options. These options will also be displayed on the order details page when you are processing your orders for shipping.

Summary

This chapter provided an overview of the administration site in nopCommerce. You learned how to access the administration site and got a detailed look at the navigation and dashboard. You walked through creating categories and manufacturers and saw the various options for configuring these pages. You learned how to add new products for your store as well as adding product variants. You saw how to set up product attributes and apply those to product variants. You also learned about checkout attributes and how those are displayed to customers in the shopping cart.

In the next chapter, you'll learn more about configuring the store and setting up payment and shipping methods.

4
Configuring the Store

nopCommerce is a fully functional e-commerce engine, and because of this there are a lot of configuration settings you can tweak. This chapter will cover some of the more important settings, or the settings you'll need to modify immediately to get your site set up correctly. Don't get overwhelmed as a lot of these settings can be left at their default state.

You can find all your store settings under the **Configuration** menu option in the administration site.

From this fly-out menu you can configure settings for all aspects of your site. The menu options with an arrow will display even more options when you hover over them. As you can see, a lot of configuration goes into a typical nopCommerce installation.

Just like the other areas of nopCommerce, you should plan to spend some time exploring all the settings in the site. Plan to go through each area of the **Configuration** section in the administration site to ensure you know all you can about your site. Sometimes there are things you didn't know were possible to achieve until you thoroughly explore the administration site!

General store settings

General store settings include things such as the base URL for your site and its name. Depending on your point of view, these may be some of the most important settings, as it effects how customers reach your site. You can view these settings by navigating to **Configuration | Settings | General and Miscellaneous Settings**. This will display the **General and Miscellaneous Settings** page:

Under the **Store information** tab are the general store settings:

- **Store name**: This is the friendly name of your store. This will be used in page titles, e-mails, and anywhere your store name is displayed.

- **Store URL**: This is the URL to the home page of your store. This URL is used for the link on the store logo, e-mails, and anywhere a link is provided for your store. It should be a base URL and should direct users to your home page.

- **Store closed**: Checking this box will display a **Store Closed** message to customers. You have the option to allow administrators to view the store as normal. This allows you to close the store to customers but allow administrators to make configuration changes to see how they would affect the store before letting customers back on the site.

- **Desktop store theme**: You can choose the store theme with this drop-down. In nopCommerce 2.8, there is only one theme to choose from, namely **Default clean**. In previous, versions there were multiple themes to choose from and you can always develop your own theme or download new ones from third-party vendors. If you have multiple themes available, you can choose one from this drop-down menu.

- **Allow customers to select a theme**: If multiple themes are available, you can allow users to choose a theme for the site. This theme would be specific to that user, so they would not be changing the theme for all users. This is on by default, but in practice it's a good idea to turn this option off so you can give your customers a consistent experience on your store.

- **Mobile devices supported**: The default nopCommerce theme includes mobile device support. Checking this box will force the site to use the mobile themes provided, which are optimized for smaller screens. Without this box checked, customers will see the default site no matter what device they are using. It's important to note that if you install a new theme, ensure it is mobile-compatible before using this option.

- **Display EU cookie law warning**: Clicking this checkbox will notify users about the use of cookies on your site. The EU Cookie Law went into action in May of 2011, and means you must obtain informed consent from customers before placing a cookie on their machine. This is for companies based in the UK only. Checking this box will display a modal window informing customers about the use of cookies on your site. They can click **OK** and the modal will not be shown to them again.

There are also other tabs on this page that allow you to control other general settings:

- **SEO settings**: You can configure some global SEO settings under this tab. You can change the **Page Title Separator** as well as the **Page Title SEO Adjustment**. This setting defines whether your store name appears before or after the page title. You can also control the default title for pages within your site.

- **Security settings**: Under this tab you can change the default encryption private key. This key is used to encrypt sensitive data in your database. It is randomly generated when you install the site, so you can leave this alone. You can also mange which administration menus are displayed to users via the ACL. Whether or not to use SSL is also under this tab. We'll cover SSL later in this chapter.

- **PDF settings**: You can manage PDF settings under this tab. PDFs are generated by the site in several locations for both internal uses as well as for customers. For instance, receipts, packing lists, invoices, and so on.

- **Localization settings**: If your site will utilize multiple languages, you can manage the settings for those here. You can choose to show images for language selections as well as whether to use SEO friendly URLs.

- **Full-Text settings**: If your database supports it, you can choose to enable full-text queries. Full-text searches can include simple words or more complex queries that include phrases. Once you enable full-text, you can choose the **Search Mode** from a drop-down list that is provided.

Payment methods

Payment methods represent the options customers have to pay you for their orders. These can include credit card payments, a check or money order, cash on delivery, and so on. nopCommerce supports both online and offline transactions, so you have a wide range of options available for accepting payments through your site.

nopCommerce also supports integration with third-party payment providers such as PayPal, Authorize.net, and Google Checkout. If you need to integrate with a third-party processor that is not currently built into nopCommerce, you can easily develop or install these into the store.

To view the current payment methods in your store, navigate to **Configuration | Payment Methods**.

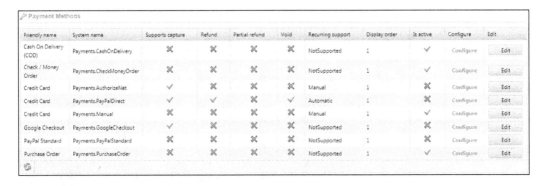

Friendly name	System name	Supports capture	Refund	Partial refund	Void	Recurring support	Display order	Is active	Configure	Edit
Cash On Delivery (COD)	Payments.CashOnDelivery	✗	✗	✗	✗	NotSupported	1	✓	Configure	Edit
Check / Money Order	Payments.CheckMoneyOrder	✗	✗	✗	✗	NotSupported	1	✓	Configure	Edit
Credit Card	Payments.AuthorizeNet	✓	✗	✗	✗	Manual	1	✗	Configure	Edit
Credit Card	Payments.PayPalDirect	✓	✓	✗	✓	Automatic	1	✗	Configure	Edit
Credit Card	Payments.Manual	✗	✗	✗	✗	Manual	1	✓	Configure	Edit
Google Checkout	Payments.GoogleCheckout	✓	✗	✗	✗	NotSupported	1	✗	Configure	Edit
PayPal Standard	Payments.PayPalStandard	✗	✗	✗	✗	NotSupported	1	✗	Configure	Edit
Purchase Order	Payments.PurchaseOrder	✗	✗	✗	✗	NotSupported	1	✓	Configure	Edit

The **Payment methods** grid lists all the payment methods installed on the site. Each payment method will display its current configuration as well as what transaction modes it supports.

- **Pending**: A transaction is pending.

- **Authorize**: This mode will authorize the card for the amount of the order. This means the credit card company is being notified that you intend to charge (capture) an amount. The site will receive a notification if the amount is available and if so, the order will be placed. You will need to capture the funds later on the order screen.

- **Authorize and Capture**: This will authorize and capture (charge) the amount of the order at the time the order is placed.

- **Void**: You can void any authorized payments that have not yet been captured.

- **Refund**: You can refund any order once it has been paid.

- **Partial Refund**: If the payment method supports it, you can partially refund an order once it has been paid.

- **Capture**: Capture is the actual charge placed on a credit card.

Not all of the payment methods shown support all of these transaction modes. Each payment method is different and may support some or all of the modes. You can see which modes are supported by configuring the payment method and inspecting its properties.

How you use these transaction modes will depend on how you operate your business. For instance, you may not want to capture (charge) a credit card until you have the order ready for shipment or the customer has picked it up. On the other hand, you may want to authorize and capture immediately before shipping to ensure the funds have been transferred to your bank account.

To configure a payment method, you can click on the **Configure** link in the grid. Depending on the payment method's configuration, you will have different options for each method.

For instance, configuring the PayPal payment method displays several options for using PayPal as well as instructions on how to set up the method:

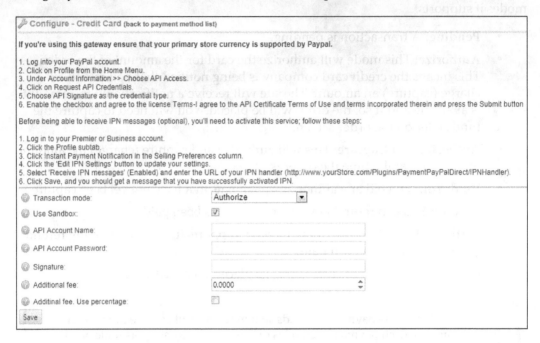

However, the purchase order payment method only has two options for its configuration:

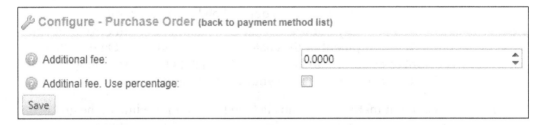

Each payment method will have different configuration options based on its needs. All of the payment methods that are preinstalled with nopCommerce will include instructions for how to set them up. The following payment methods are preinstalled:

- Manual processing (Credit Cards)
- Authorize.net
- PayPal Standard

- PayPal Direct (PayPal Pro)
- Cash on Delivery
- Purchase Order
- Google Checkout

Shipping

Shipping plays a big role in any e-commerce store that sells shippable products. How you decide to ship your products is based on your business needs, but customers today expect to have different shipping options available to them. These include ground, priority, and express. nopCommerce gives you excellent control over how to set up shipping on your site and manage its features and pricing.

Shipping Methods

Shipping methods represent the levels of shipping a customer can choose from when checking out, that is, ground, priority, express, and so on. You can view the current shipping methods for your site by navigating to **Configuration | Shipping | Shipping Methods**:

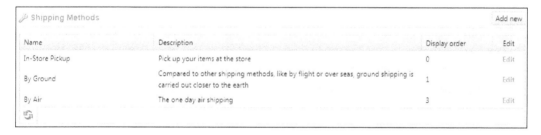

You can edit a shipping method by clicking on the **Edit** link in the grid. You can also add new methods by clicking on the **Add New** button. The **Name** property is shown to the customer when selecting their shipping level. The shipping methods grid only allows you to specify your shipping levels. You can specify the rate charged for these methods under **Shipping Rate Computation Methods**.

These methods are considered "offline" shipping methods. If you are using a real time shipping rate such as UPS, USPS, FedEx, and so on, these methods will not apply and will not be shown to the user. This is not to say you cannot use a service such as UPS with these methods, but the pricing would be fixed or by weight rather than real time.

Shipping method restrictions

You can also restrict which methods are allowed to ship where. For instance, if you ship to the U.S. and Canada, but do not want to allow air shipments to Canada, you can restrict that method for that area. To view your shipping method restrictions, navigate to **Configuration | Shipping | Shipping Method Restrictions**:

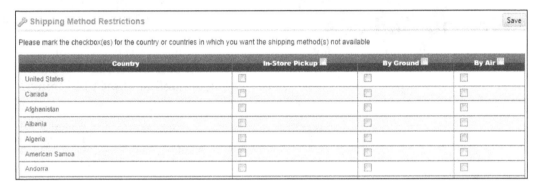

In the **Shipping Method Restrictions** grid, you can check the countries and shipping methods you want to restrict.

Shipping rate computation methods

Shipping rate computation methods are how you define how much to charge for each shipping method. This area is also where you can view all the shipping providers that are installed on your site. To view these, navigate to **Configuration** | **Shipping** | **Shipping Rate Computation Methods**:

Friendly name	System name	Display order	Is active	Configure	Edit
Australia Post	Shipping.AustraliaPost	1	✕	Configure	Edit
Canada Post	Shipping.CanadaPost	1	✕	Configure	Edit
FedEx	Shipping.FedEx	1	✕	Configure	Edit
Fixed Rate Shipping	Shipping.FixedRate	1	✓	Configure	Edit
Shipping by weight	Shipping.ByWeight	1	✕	Configure	Edit
UPS (United Parcel Service)	Shipping.UPS	1	✕	Configure	Edit
USPS (US Postal Service)	Shipping.USPS	1	✕	Configure	Edit

nopCommerce has two different kinds of shipping providers: **Offline** and **Real Time**. Offline providers include **Fixed Rate Shipping** and **Shipping by Weight**. These are offline in the sense that they will use settings found within your site to determine what to charge a customer for their shipping. Real Time providers include UPS, USPS, FedEx, and so on. These are "real time" since they will communicate with the provider's servers to determine a current rate to charge the customer.

 Only one "offline" shipping provider should be active at any given time. If you mark one as **Is Active**, ensure you mark the others as not active to avoid issues for your customers when checking out.

Shipping by weight

If you would like to calculate shipping charges based on the weight of the shipment, choose this provider. This is useful if you sell heavy products that can be expensive to ship. To set up shipping by weight, edit the provider in the **Shipping Rate Computation Methods** grid and mark it as **Is Active**. You can then configure the provider by clicking the **Configure** link.

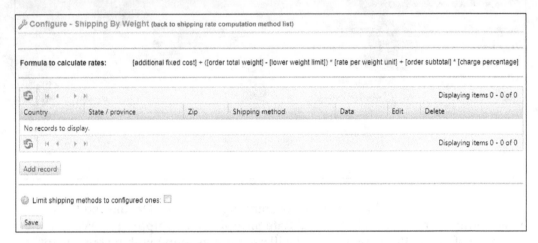

The **Limit shipping methods to configured ones** checkbox allows you to limit shipping options to only those configured here. Otherwise, customers will be able to choose any existing shipping options even if they are not configured here.

Click on the **Add Record** button to add a new shipping by weight row:

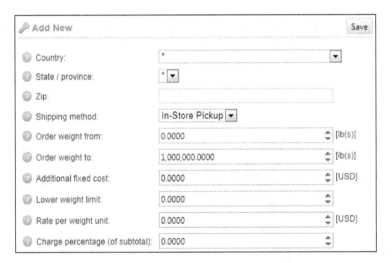

- **Country**: Select the country from the drop-down list. Selecting * will make the rate apply to all countries.
- **State/Province**: Select the state/province from the drop-down list. Selecting * will make the rate apply to all states/provinces for the selected country.
- **Zip**: Enter the zip/postal code. You can leave this blank and the rate will apply to all codes under that state/province.
- **Shipping method**: Select the shipping method from the drop-down list. These are the shipping methods that were defined earlier.
- **Order weight from** and **Order weight to**: Enter the weight range you would like this rate to apply to.
- **Additional fixed cost**: You can opt to charge an additional fee for a certain rate. For instance, if the weight range is the heaviest you offer to ship, you may need to charge a little extra to cover your costs.
- **Lower weight limit**: You can enter a lower weight limit here. This value will be used for "per extra weight limit scenarios".
- **Rate per weight unit**: This is the rate charged per unit of weight.
- **Charge percentage of subtotal**: This value will be used to charge a percentage of the subtotal.

All these values are used in the following calculation:

[additional fixed cost] + ([order total weight] - [lower weight limit]) * [rate per weight unit] + [order subtotal] * [charge percentage].

This formula is used to calculate the shipping charge when using the shipping by weight method.

Fixed rate shipping

If you would like to calculate shipping charges based on fixed rates by shipping method, choose this provider. This is the easiest shipping provider as you simply give a fixed rate to each shipping level. To set up fixed rate shipping, edit the provider in the **Shipping Rate Computation Methods** grid and mark it as **Is Active**. You can then configure the provider by clicking on the **Configure** link:

Configure - Fixed Rate Shipping (back to shipping rate computation method list)		
Shipping method	Rate	Edit
In-Store Pickup	0.00	Edit
By Ground	0.00	Edit
By Air	0.00	Edit

The shipping methods displayed in the grid are the methods that were configured in the **Shipping Methods** area. You can click on the **Edit** button in the row and then modify the **Rate**. You can enter in a dollar amount for the shipping method.

> **Real world**: A large majority of e-commerce sites utilize fixed rate shipping. This can be for a lot of reasons, but by far it will make managing your shipping options easy. Take some time to explore all the options available to you and make sure you are choosing a shipping provider that provides ease of use as well as cost savings. These need to be balanced when making this decision.

In addition to offline shipping providers, nopCommerce comes with several real time shipping rate providers out of the box. These include: USPS, UPS, FedEx, Canada Post, and Australia Post.

This book will not cover how to set up each one of these providers, but they all have several things in common:

- **API Account**: In order to communicate with their servers to obtain real time rate information, you will need to obtain an API account with the provider. For instance, with UPS you will be given a URL to access the service, an access key, a username, and a password. This information will be needed to properly configure the UPS shipping provider. No matter which real time provider you use, similar information will be required that can only be obtained by creating an account with the provider.
- **Shipping Methods**: Each provider has a selection of shipping levels that you can offer. You will need to select which shipping methods from the provider you wish to offer your customers.

Taxes

If your business is e-commerce only, you will most likely need to collect some taxes. Depending on where your business is located, your tax laws may vary, but nopCommerce gives you all the tools necessary to properly collect taxes on your sales.

Real world: It's very important that you stay informed with tax collection. E-commerce laws are changing with regards to when and where taxes must be collected. Gone are the days of being able to run your e-commerce site without worrying about paying taxes on sales. If your business is US-based, you will at the very least need to collect taxes for the state you are located in. Check your local, state, and federal tax laws to ensure you are complying with them.

nopCommerce gives you the ability to configure taxes by categories and/or by locations. With this ability you can tax orders shipped to certain areas by their location as well as by the type of product. This gives you the ability to collect the correct amount of tax on all of your orders.

Tax categories

Tax categories can be created and then assigned to products, shipping, and so on. This will later allow you to charge additional taxes if needed. You can view all your current tax categories by navigating to **Configuration | Tax | Tax Categories**:

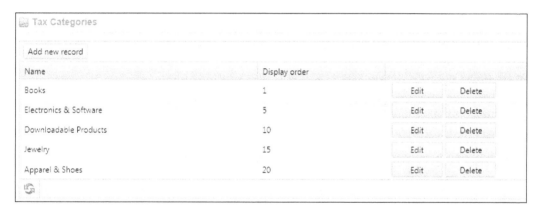

This page allows you to add or edit tax categories only. The actual tax rates that apply to these categories are set up under the **Tax Providers** area. You can add a new tax category by clicking on the **Add New Record** button. Editing current categories is done inline in the grid.

Tax providers

nopCommerce comes with two tax providers out of the box: **Fixed Rate Tax** and **Tax by Country & State & Zip**. You can view the current tax providers by navigating to **Configuration | Tax | Tax Providers**:

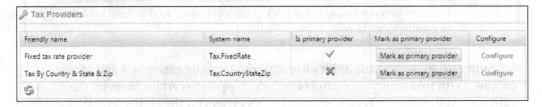

 Only one tax provider may be active at any given time. Make sure you choose the one that best suits your needs. You can change the current provider by clicking on the **Mark as primary provider** button in the grid.

The **Fixed Rate Tax** provider utilizes the categories that are set up under **Tax Categories**. This allows you to tax products using a flat tax based on the category of the product. When configuring your products, you can specify which tax category applies to them, and this is the rate at which they will be taxed. To specify the rates, click on the **Configure** link for the **Fixed Rate Tax Provider**:

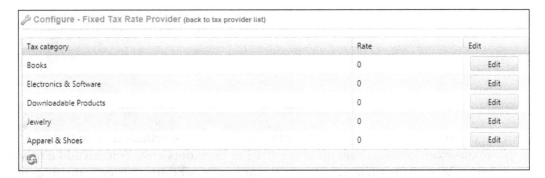

The grid that displays contains all the tax categories that were set up previously. You can click on the **Edit** button in the row to update the tax rate for the category.

Tax by Country & State & Zip is used to calculate taxes by the country, state, and zip code of where the order is shipping. To view the current regions set up for this provider, click on the **Configure** link in the grid:

In a default installation of nopCommerce, no regions are set up yet for this provider. To add a new region, fill out the information below the grid and click on the **Add tax rate** button.

- **Country**: Select the country for the region.
- **State/province**: Select the state or province the tax rate applies to. Selecting * will make the rate apply to all states/provinces for the selected country.
- **Zip**: Enter the zip/postal code for the region. You can leave this blank and the rate will apply to all codes under that state/province.
- **Tax category**: Select the tax category.
- **Percentage**: Enter the percentage applied for this region.

> **Real world**: If your site is based in the U.S., you most likely will just have one region defined here, the state in which you are running the business. Most small e-commerce sites generally only have their online store or maybe some brick and mortar locations in the same state, and thus only need to collect taxes for their state. Check your local, state, and federal tax laws to ensure you are complying with all tax laws.

You can also add third-party tax rate providers to your site. Additional tax rate providers can be downloaded from the nopCommerce site and include Strike Iron and Avalara.

Content management

Content management in nopCommerce includes several different areas in your store. These areas include blogs, polls, forums, widgets, news, topics, and message templates. In this section, we'll be going into detail on the **Topics**, **Email Accounts**, and **Message Templates** areas. These areas of content management are the ones you'll be using most often, but it's worth reviewing the other areas:

- **Blog**: nopCommerce comes with a built-in blog engine. To edit or add new posts, you can navigate to **Content Management | Blog | Blog Posts**. This will display a grid with all your current posts.

  You can edit posts here by clicking on the **Edit** link or add new posts by clicking on the **Add New** button. You can also view any comments on your blog posts by navigating to **Content Management | Blog | Blog Comments**. To view the blog, you can navigate to http://www.yourdomain.com/blog.

  By default, the blog is enabled. You can turn off the blog by navigating to **Configuration | Settings | Blog Settings** and un-checking the **Blog Enabled** setting.

  > **Real world**: The blog engine in nopCommerce is great and can definitely serve the blogging needs of your site. However, if you plan on heavily using a blog as a marketing tool, you may consider a third-party engine such as WordPress.

- **Polls**: You can set up and manage polls to interact with your users. You can view the current polls you have set up by navigating to **Content Management | Polls**. This will display a grid with all the polls on your site. Polls will appear in the left-hand side area of the site, under the navigation. You can also specify if you want the poll to show up on the home page of the site.

- **Forums**: Forums allow you to interact with your customers and allow them to interact with each other. nopCommerce comes with a built-in forums engine. By default, the forums are disabled, but you can turn them on by navigating to **Configuration | Settings | Forum Settings** and checking the **Forums Enabled** setting. After this you can view your forums by navigating to http://www.yourdomain.com/boards.

- **Widgets**: Widgets provide a way to insert new functionality into your site without changing the code. A default installation of nopCommerce includes two widgets: **Google Analytics** and **Nivo Slider**. You can view these by navigating to **Content Management | Widgets**. This will display all the widgets currently installed on your site. Widgets can be placed in predefined zones in your **Layout** pages, for instance, the left or right column. They can also be non-visible aspects of your site such as the Google Analytics widget. You can also download third-party widgets or develop your own to enhance your site.

- **News**: News acts like a scaled down blog and has a similar appearance to a blog, but is quite different. Users can view news for the store by clicking on the **News** link on the home page. The news displays a short snippet of information and the customer can click on the **Details** link to view the full article. When viewing the full news article, there is a section that allows for comments to be placed.

  You can manage all your news content by navigating to **Content Management | News | News Items**. This will display a grid of all the news items you currently have on the site. If you have opted to allow comments on your news items, you can view any that have been left by navigating to **Content Management | News | News Comments**. This will display a grid of all the current news comments. You can delete comments here to remove them from news items.

Topics (Pages)

Topics (Pages) are ancillary pages that you can use to show content other than products. Common pages include **About Us**, **Contact Us**, **Shipping Information**, and so on. You can add as many topics as you like, and you have complete control over the content displayed there.

Topics can be either full pages that you access via a URL, or they can be used to display content embedded within other pages using code. These are great for quickly adding new content to your site without needing to develop new pages.

To view all the current topics in your site, navigate to **Content Management | Topics (Pages)**. This will display a grid of all the topics:

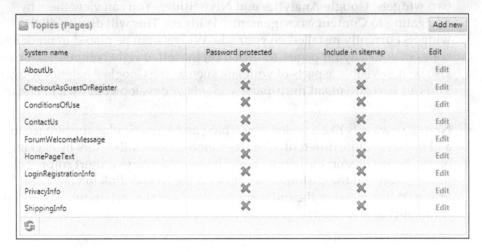

Topics have a uniform URL that you access them with, `http://www.yourdomain.com/t/systemname`. To reach the **About Us** page, your URL would be `http://www.yourdomain.com/t/aboutus`, since the **About Us** page has a system name of `AboutUs`. You can add a new topic by clicking on the **Add New** button in the top-right:

- **System name**: This is the name the site uses to figure out which topic to display. It will be part of the URL and cannot contain any spaces or special characters.

- **Password protected**: You can opt to password protect any topic page. This is useful if you have a certain group of users that you want to show special information too, but keep out of sight to everyone else. Checking this box will display a **Password** textbox so you can supply a password for this page.

- **Include in sitemap**: Check this box if you would like to include this page in the sitemap.

- **Title**: This is the title of the topic that will be displayed to the user.

- **Body**: This is a full HTML editor where you can put the content of your topic. This is the main content of the page and will be displayed below the topic title.

Email accounts

Email accounts are used to send e-mails from the site to customers and you, the store owner. You can add as many e-mail accounts as you like, and these are used in conjunction with the message templates to send mail, as described below in **Content Management**.

To view the e-mail addresses you have added, navigate to **Content Management | Email Accounts**:

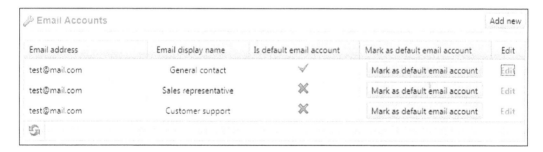

One e-mail account will always be marked as the default account. This account will be used if no other account is specified when sending e-mails. You can change which address is the default account by clicking on the **Mark as default email account** button.

You can add a new e-mail account by clicking on the **Add New** button:

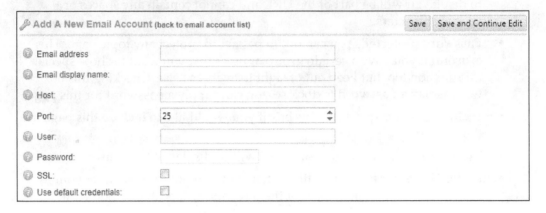

- **Email address**: This is the e-mail address the account should use for outgoing e-mails, for example, `customerservice@yourdomain.com`.

- **Email display name**: The display name is the name that will display as the **From** field in the e-mail.

- **Host** and **Port**: This is the IP or hostname of your e-mail server. You can work with your hosting provider for this information, but typically it looks like `email.yourdomain.com`. **Port** is the SMTP port number of the e-mail server.

- **User** and **Password**: This is the username and password for the e-mail account on your e-mail server.

- **SSL**: Check this box to enable SSL and encrypt the SMTP connection. Check with your hosting provider if this is required.

- **Use default credentials**: Check this if you need to authenticate using the default credentials of the currently logged-on user. Typically this should not be checked.

Once you have saved the new account, you will see a new section from where you can send a test e-mail. This allows you to test the new account to ensure it was set up properly:

Enter a valid e-mail address and click on the **Send test email** button. The site will generate a test e-mail that simply states that the e-mail functionality is working.

Message templates

Message templates represent e-mails that are generated by the site. These e-mails can either be directed to your customers or to you as the storeowner. They include messages such as **Order Confirmation**, **New Customer Notification**, **Email a Friend**, **News Comment**, and so on. When the site sends a new e-mail, it will generate the content based on the message template. The templates contain static text as well as variables for content, for instance, the new order notification contains a variable to display all the order line items.

Real world: You should take the time to get familiar with all the messages your site generates as well as customize the templates. E-mails are a great way to market to your customers. Order notifications, email a friend, and so on, are e-mails that customers are generally happy to receive and will open without hesitation. Adding logos, contact information, marketing banners, and so on to your e-mails will go a long way to keep you site in the minds of current and prospective customers.

You can view all the message templates in your site by navigating to **Content Management | Message Templates**:

Name	Subject	Is active	Edit
Blog.BlogComment	%Store.Name%. New blog comment.	✓	Edit
Customer.BackInStock	%Store.Name%. Back in stock notification	✓	Edit
Customer.EmailValidationMessage	%Store.Name%. Email validation	✓	Edit
Customer.NewOrderNote	%Store.Name%. New order note has been added	✓	Edit
Customer.NewPM	%Store.Name%. You have received a new private message	✓	Edit
Customer.PasswordRecovery	%Store.Name%. Password recovery	✓	Edit
Customer.WelcomeMessage	Welcome to %Store.Name%	✓	Edit

There are quite a few message templates built into nopCommerce. The grid that is shown in the preceding screenshot gives you some quick information about each template, most importantly the e-mail's subject line and shows if it is active. You can edit any template by clicking on the **Edit** link in the grid.

- **Allowed message tokens**: Message tokens are the variables used in the e-mail message. They have a uniform format of %TokenName% and will be replaced by the site when the e-mail is generated. For instance, the %Order. Product(s)% token will render all the line items for a customer's order in a table format. Not all tokens are available for all message templates. If the site generates a new blog comment e-mail, then all of the order tokens will not have data in them. Keep this in mind when modifying your templates.

- **Name**: This is the system name of the message template and is used by the site to use the proper template when generating e-mails.

- **Is Active**: You can disable templates and e-mails from being generated by unchecking this box.

- **BCC**: You can blind carbon copy an e-mail that is sent from the site by providing an address in this field. This is very useful for e-mails such as **Email a Friend**, as you may want to keep track of what people of recommending to their friends.

- **Subject**: This is the subject line of the e-mail. The subject line can include tokens and/or static text. When using tokens, be careful not to use a token that generates more than a single line of text.

- **Body**: This is a full HTML editor where you can craft the e-mail body. You will use tokens heavily in here. This is also where you can add in your logo or other information you want to appear in your e-mails. When working with the message templates, it's a good idea to open all your templates and review their structure, as this will help enormously when modifying your templates.

- **Email account**: This drop-down lists all the e-mail accounts you have set up on your site. You can choose which e-mail account to use when sending an e-mail based on this template.

When you open the **Message Templates** page, you will notice there is no way to add a new template from the administration site. You can add new templates to the site but only by inserting them into the database directly. In addition, once you have a new template loaded, you will need to develop custom code to be able to send e-mails using the new template. However, the templates that come with nopCommerce represent everything you will need to get started.

> **Real world**: Most likely you will not need a new message template for your site. The templates that come with a base installation are comprehensive and generally more than what a typical site needs. If you do find you need another template, adding one is not difficult, but will require a developer to modify the code.

Plugins

You can extend the functionality of nopCommerce by installing and configuring plugins. Plugins include things such as discounts, shipping methods, tax providers, and widgets. You can download third-party plugins and install them to your site without the need for custom code. You can also develop your own plugins if the need arises. For instance, imagine you need to accept your own in-house credit card for payments. You can develop your own payment method plugin, install it on your site, and make it available as a payment option on your site. This framework opens up a lot of possibilities for your site.

The base installation of nopCommerce comes with a wide range of plugins that are ready to use. These include payment methods such as PayPal and Google Checkout, as well as shipping methods such as FedEx and UPS. To view all the plugins that are currently installed, navigate to **Configuration | Plugins**:

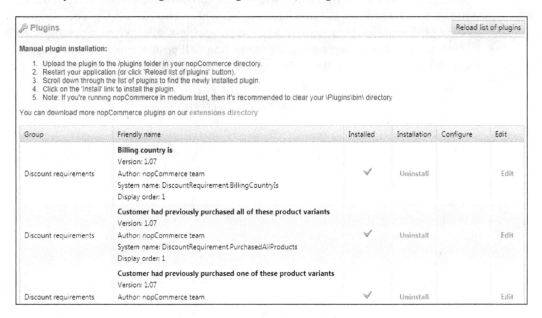

The **Group** column is important as it tells you what type of plugin this is. The grid will also list whether the plugin is currently installed.

Installing new plugins is quite easy, just follow these steps:

1. Once you have developed or downloaded a new plugin, upload it to the /Plugins folder, which is located in the root of your site. You will see folders for all the plugins you currently have installed:

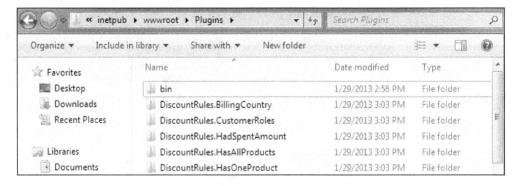

2. Once you have uploaded the plugin, return to the plugins page in the administration site and click on the **Reload List of Plugins** button at the top-right.

3. Locate the plugin in the grid and click on the **Install** link.

4. If the plugin supports configuration, you can then click on the **Configure** link.

Once you have installed a plugin, you can easily uninstall it by clicking on the **Uninstall** link in the grid.

Security (SSL)

Secure Sockets Layer (SSL) is an industry-standard security technology that encrypts data passing between a web server and a browser. You know you're using a secured site with SSL when the URL contains `https`. Just about every e-commerce site on the Internet utilizes SSL communications to ensure credit card information is passed in a secured way. Your site is no different. If you plan on taking credit card payments, you must ensure you have SSL set up and configured to protect your customers and yourself.

Before you can enable SSL on your site, you will need to obtain an SSL certificate. These can be purchased from a variety of vendors such as `GoDaddy.com` or your hosting provider. I won't go into detail about how to purchase and set up a certificate in this book, but you will have to work with your hosting provider to install the certificate once you have purchased one.

You can enable SSL on your site in two ways:

- Enable via the administration site: In the administration site, navigate to **Configuration | Settings | General and Miscellaneous Settings**. Under the **Security settings** tab, check the box titled **Use SSL**. This will update the site's `web.config` file for you to enable SSL:

SSL settings
SSL settings can also be changed in web.config file.

Use SSL:	☑
Shared SSL URL:	
Non-secured URL:	

If you are using a shared SSL certificate, you will need to enter that information. Shared SSL gives you get the benefits of SSL without the costs that are usually associated with setting up an SSL server. With this option you use your hosting provider's SSL certificate and typically get a secure URL such as `https://secure.yourdomain.com`. The non-secured URL is typically your domain name, for example, `http://www.yourdomain.com`.

- Manually enable via the `web.config` file: You can also enable SSL by updating your `web.config` file. The SSL settings can be found in the **AppSettings** section.

> It's important to remember that enabling SSL in the administration site is updating the `web.config` file. The reason this is important is if you are doing any custom development. If the `web.config` you are uploading to the site does not have the correct settings, you will effectively turn off SSL inadvertently. Make sure your `web.config` file used in development is configured properly before uploading any site changes.

Once you've enabled SSL any pages that require a secure connection will begin using the `https` protocol.

Summary

This chapter covered a lot of material. nopCommerce has many settings, so you can configure your store to meet your exact needs. You learned about general store settings which are used throughout the entire storefront. You also learned about payment methods and how to configure the out-of-the-box providers. You looked at how shipping is configured in nopCommerce and learned how to configure shipping to meet your needs. You learned about collecting taxes and content management. You saw the plugins framework and learned how it can help extend your store without writing custom code.

In the next chapter, you'll learn how to process and manage the orders customers place on your site.

5
Processing Orders

Your storefront is set up and now the orders are rolling in! Well, that's at least what the goal is, but once you start receiving orders, you'll need to process them to get the products out to your customers. nopCommerce makes processing orders relatively simple and gives you all the tools you need. We've already covered the **Dashboard** page in the *How to access and overview* section of *Chapter 3*, *The Administration Site*, which gives you a quick overview of the orders you've received. Now we'll dig deeper into the sales area where you will be working to process all your orders.

Processing orders

You can view all of your orders by navigating to **Sales | Orders**:

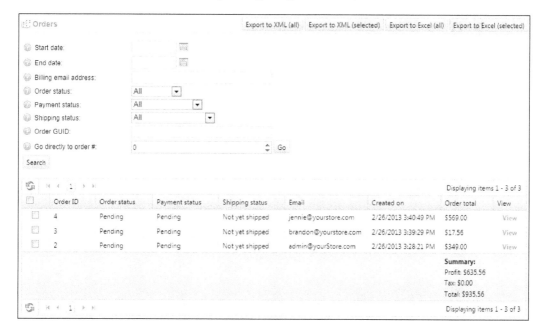

The orders page displays all the orders in a paged grid. There is a **Summary** section under the grid that displays totals for all your orders. These totals include:

- **Profit**: This total is the difference between the gross total and the total cost of products sold without tax included. It's important to note that this is a high-level profit total, since it simply looks at the cost entered for your products. Depending on how you account for product cost (shipping, marketing, holding costs, and so on), this profit total may not represent a true number for your business.

- **Tax**: This is a total of all the tax collected for all your orders.

- **Total**: This is a gross total of all your orders without tax included.

This grid will display all orders regardless of their status. You can use the filters above the grid to search for specific orders:

- **Start date** and **End date**: Enter a start and end date to search for orders within a certain date range.

- **Billing email address**: Enter the customer's billing e-mail address to search for orders by a certain user.

- **Order status**: Select an order status from the drop-down list. Order statuses include **All, Pending, Processing, Complete**, and **Cancelled**.

- **Payment status**: Select a payment status from the drop-down list. Payment statuses include **All, Pending, Authorized, Paid, Refunded, Partially refunded**, and **Voided**.

- **Shipping status**: Select a shipping status from the drop-down list. Shipping statuses include **All, Shipping not required, Not yet shipped, Partially shipped, Shipped**, and **Delivered**.

- **Order GUID**: You can search by entering the order's **Global Unique Identifier (GUID)** or a partial GUID. This is an internal ID, not the order number the customer sees.

- **Go directly to order number**: Technically, this is not a search option, as you are going straight to a particular order number. You can enter an order number here and click **Go**. This will take you directly to the order details page.

You can click on the **View** link in the grid to view a particular order's details:

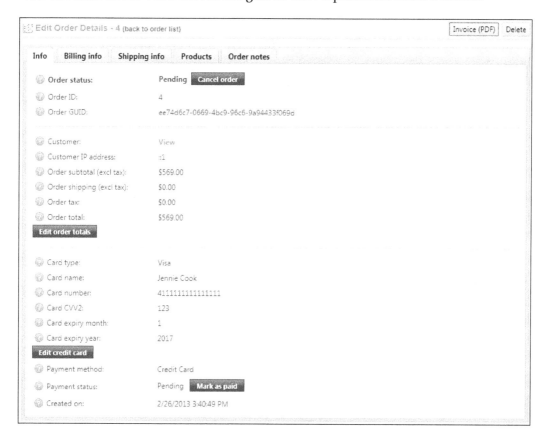

The preceding screenshot shows an order that was placed using the **Manual Credit Card** provider. This provider stores credit card information in the database and allows you to update the credit card number the customer provided. If you use another credit card provider, such as PayPal, this option will not be available.

On the orders details page, you can view all aspects of the order under the various tabs.

Viewing and editing order information

In the order status area, you can view the status, order ID, and GUID. You can cancel an order here by clicking on the **Cancel Order** button. You will get a confirmation prompt to ensure you really want to cancel the order.

In the order totals area, you can view the total, subtotal, tax, and shipping amounts for the order. You can update these totals by clicking on the **Edit order totals** button. You can also view the customer by clicking on the **View** link.

In the payment area, you can view information about the payment method used. The information displayed here will vary based on the payment method used. The payment status field will display the current payment status. Depending on the payment method used, you may have additional action buttons here, such as **Refund**, **Capture**, and **Void**. If it's displayed, you click the **Mark as paid** button to set the order as **Paid**.

Viewing and editing order billing information

The **Billing info** tab will display the address the customer entered as their billing address. You can click on the **Edit** button to update the billing address for this customer:

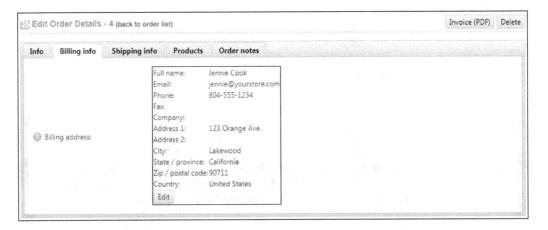

Viewing and editing order shipping information

The **Shipping info** tab will display the address the customer entered as their shipping address. You can click on the **Edit** button to update the shipping address for this customer:

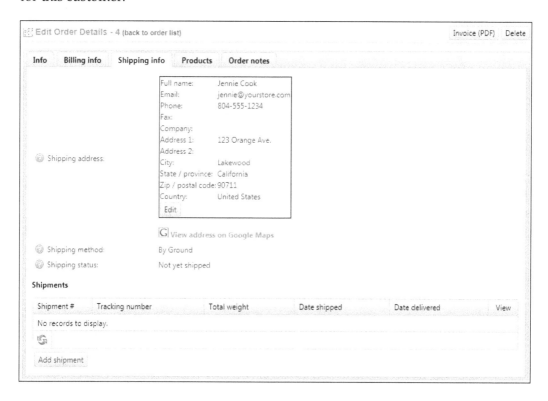

This tab will also display the shipping method selected by the customer as well as the shipping status for the order. You can click on the **View address on Google Maps** link to open a new window that will display the address on a map.

You can also manage shipments for the order from under this tab. Click on the **Add shipment** button to launch the **Add a New Shipment to Order** page:

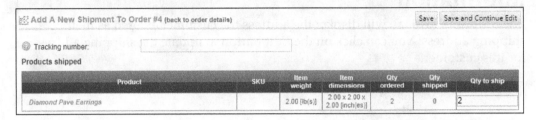

On this page, you can enter a tracking number and specify the quantities of the product in this shipment. nopCommerce supports multiple shipments, so if your shipment does not contain all the products in the order, you will be able to add shipments until all the products are shipped. Once you have shipped all the products, the **Add shipment** button will no longer be displayed.

Once a shipment has been entered, the shipping status of the order is updated. If you do not ship all the products in one shipment, the status will be updated to **Partially shipped**. Once all the items have been shipped, the status will change to **Shipped**.

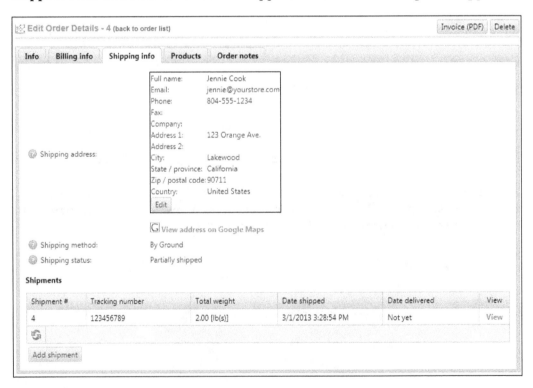

Once shipments have been added to an order, you can click on the **View** link in the **Shipments** grid to view/update the shipping information:

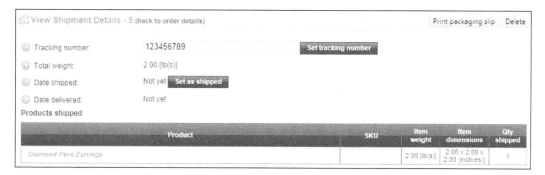

You can print a packing slip by clicking on the **Print packing slip** button. This is a very minimal document that contains the shipping address, shipping method, and a grid with all the items that are included with the shipment. If you need to update the tracking number, you can enter the new number here and click **Set tracking number**.

Before the customer will be notified of a shipment, you will need to click the **Set as shipped** button. This will update the shipping status on the order as well as generate an e-mail to notify the customer. You can see these updates under the **Order notes** tab.

In addition to working with shipments via the customer's order, you can also view all the shipments you have entered by navigating to **Sales | Shipments**:

You can narrow the results displayed in the grid by specifying a start and end date above and clicking on the **Search** button. Just like in the **Shipping** tab, you can click on the **View** link to view the details of any shipment.

Viewing and editing ordered products

This tab displays a grid that contains all the products the customer ordered:

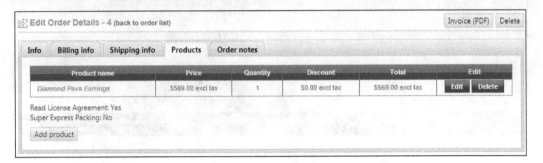

 Any checkout attributes you have set up for your store will display in this tab. These attributes will display directly below the products grid. If you do not have any checkout attributes defined, you will not see any information here.

You can click the product name in the grid to be taken to the product variant page in the administration site. If the item is a downloadable product, you will have some additional options listed here:

- **Activate**: If the product is manually downloaded by the customer, you will have the option to activate or deactivate the download

- **License file**: This is an optional field; you can upload a license file for the downloadable product by clicking on **Upload License File**

In the products grid, each line item will display **Edit** and **Delete** buttons. You can edit the details of the product including price, quantity, and total. Clicking **Delete** will remove the product from the order.

You can also add products to an existing order via the **Products** tab. Click on the **Add product** button to display the **Add a New Product to Order** screen:

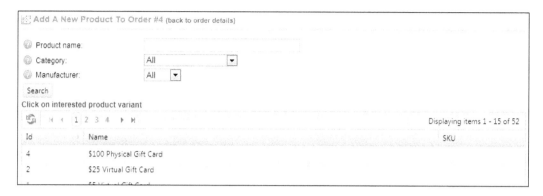

You can search for the product you want to add using the options above the grid. Once you locate the product, click the product in the grid; this will launch the add product window:

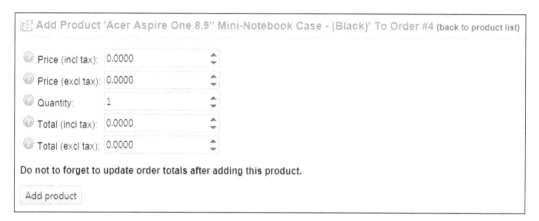

Fill out the required information and click **Add product**.

Adding and deleting order notes

You can add notes to any order in the store and view these under the **Order notes** tab. These notes can be for anything, and some are auto-generated by the store and added for you:

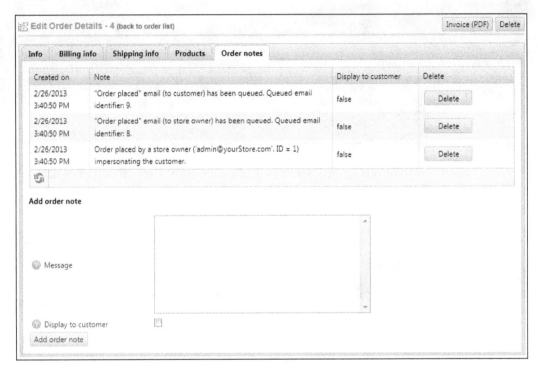

The notes grid will display all the current notes attached to the order. You can delete a note at any time by clicking on the **Delete** button. You can add new notes by filling out the information below the grid:

- **Message**: Enter any information you would like to attach to this order.
- **Display to customer**: Check this box if you would like the note to be displayed to the customer. Customers can view order notes via the order details page in their account. The grid also displays if the note is available for the customer to view.

Click on **Add order note** to add the new note.

Processing returns

nopCommerce allows customers to submit return requests on orders. This is a very useful feature in that it allows customers to submit and view the process of their returns without needing to contact you — the storeowner — for support. Return requests are only available for orders that are marked **Completed**. Only after this status is assigned to the order will the customer be able to submit a request.

Return requests are enabled by default, but you can turn this feature off via the administration site. You can also manage other settings as well. To view the return request settings, navigate to **Configuration | Settings | Order Settings**. On the **Order settings** page, click on the **Return request settings** tab:

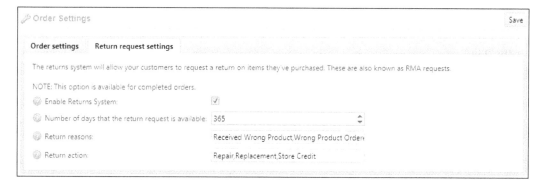

- **Enable Returns System**: Check this box to enable return requests. This is enabled by default.

- **Number of days that the return request is available**: Set the number of days from the order date that returns will be accepted. For instance, if you have a 14 day return policy, set this value to 14. After 14 days from the order date, the customer will no longer see a return button when viewing their order details.

- **Return reasons**: This is a list of reasons the customer may be returning their order. These reasons will be presented to the customer as a drop-down list when filling out the request. Reasons must be separated by commas.

- **Return action**: This is a list of actions the customer may request for the return, that is, **Replace, Credit, Exchange**, and so on. These actions will be presented to the customer as a drop-down list when filling out the request. Actions must be separated by commas.

Once the customer's order status has been set to **Completed**, they will have the option to request a return by clicking on the **Return item(s)** button when viewing orders in their account:

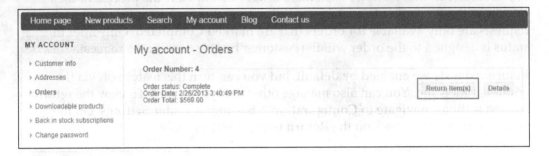

Clicking on the **Return item(s)** button will launch the **Return item(s) from order** page:

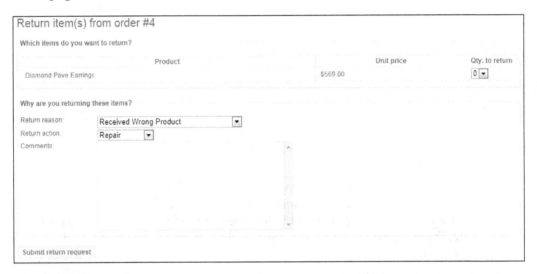

The customer can choose the quantity they are returning and pick **Return reason** and **Return action** from the options you have defined in the administration site. They can also provide comments about the return. Once the customer clicks on the **Submit return request** button, the request is submitted. Customers can track their requests in their account under the **Return requests** section:

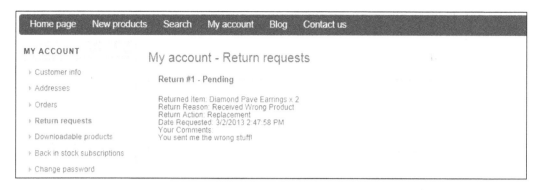

To view all the return requests that customers have submitted, navigate to
Sales | Return Requests in the administration site:

From this grid, you can view the customer and/or order related to the request.
To view and process the return, click on the **Edit** link for the request. This will
launch the **Edit Return Request Details** page:

- **ID**: This is simply the internal ID for the return request.

- **Product**: You can click this link to go to the product variant for the returned product.

- **Quantity**: This is the quantity the customer entered for the request.

- **Order** and **Customer**: These links will take you to the order and customer pages if you need to view any additional details.

- **Return request status**: You can change the status of the request with this drop-down. The available options include: **Pending, Received, Return Authorized, Item(s) Repaired, Item(s) Refunded, Request Rejected**, and **Cancelled**. These statuses will be displayed to the customer in their account when viewing their return requests.

- **Reason for return** and **Request action**: These are the options the customer chose when submitting the request.

- **Customer comments**: These are the comments the customer entered. Any changes you make here will show up on the return request the customer views in their account.

- **Staff notes**: These are internal notes for staff. These will not be displayed to the customer.

- **Date**: This is the timestamp the return request was submitted by the customer.

Any updates/edits you make on this page will not automatically notify the customer. You can click on the **Notify customer about status change** button on the top-right of the page to do this. This will generate an e-mail to the customer that simply states that the status of the request has been changed. The e-mail will not include any other information; the customer will need to log in to their account to view the updated status.

If the outcome of the return is a refund, you will need to update the order and perform a refund. The return request pages do not make any changes to orders; these actions will need to be performed manually.

Viewing current shopping carts and wishlists

nopCommerce gives you the ability to view all the current shopping carts and wishlists for your store. This will show you the items that customers have added to these areas but have not yet purchased.

To view the current shopping carts, navigate to **Sales | Current Shopping Carts**:

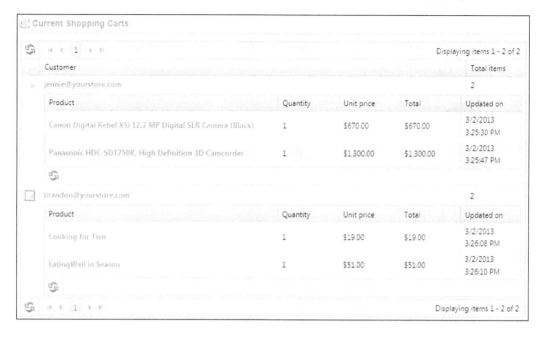

The grid will display a list of all the customers who have a current shopping cart. You can click the arrow next to the customer e-mail to expand the cart and see its contents. You can see each product in the cart as well as the quantity the customer entered. The **Updated on** column will display the last activity date for the cart. The current wishlist page has the exact same format, and information and can be viewed by navigating to **Sales | Current Wishlists**.

Real world: You may ask yourself why this information is important. This information can be used in many different ways. From a marketing perspective, you could develop some code that would e-mail customers with a coupon code to complete their order if their shopping cart does not update after X number of days. You may also get some insight into your customer's behavior as well. If, for instance, you saw a lot of people adding a particular product but never buying it, you may look into changing its product description, lowering its price, or running a sale.

Impersonating a customer

If you intend to have a phone number for your site and interact with customers via the phone, you may find yourself in a position to place an order for a customer. Luckily, nopCommerce has this ability built-in. If your customer has an account, you can impersonate them and place an order for them. This allows you to act on behalf of the customer without the need of their password.

To impersonate a customer, navigate to **Customers | Customers**. Locate the customer you would like to impersonate and click on the **Edit** link in the grid. On the **Edit Customer Details** page, click on the **Place order (Impersonate)** tab:

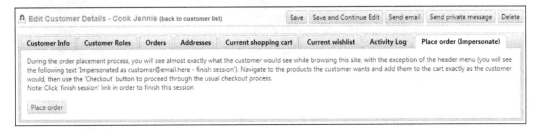

Click on the **Place order** button to begin impersonating the customer. You will be taken to the home page of your store with a header that indicates you are impersonating a customer, as shown here:

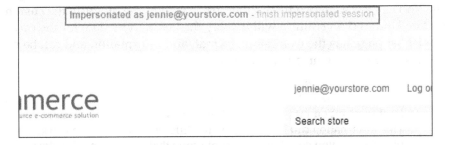

While in impersonation mode, you can use the site just as a normal customer would. The only difference during this time is the header. You can add products and checkout through the usual process. When you are finished, click on the **finish impersonated session** link in the header. This will take you back to the customer details screen where you were prior.

Summary

In this chapter, you learned how to process orders. You got an overview of all the components of a customer's order, from the billing and shipping details down to the products ordered. You learned how to manipulate orders and add notes for future reference. You saw how to process returns, as well as how to view current shopping carts and place orders for customers.

You now have a solid grasp on setting up and running your own storefront using nopCommerce. You've seen how to download and install, set up your store, and manage orders. You are now ready to start running your own storefront and make money using nopCommerce.

Index

Thank you for buying
Getting Started with nopCommerce

About Packt Publishing

Packt, pronounced 'packed', published its first book "*Mastering phpMyAdmin for Effective MySQL Management*" in April 2004 and subsequently continued to specialize in publishing highly focused books on specific technologies and solutions.

Our books and publications share the experiences of your fellow IT professionals in adapting and customizing today's systems, applications, and frameworks. Our solution based books give you the knowledge and power to customize the software and technologies you're using to get the job done. Packt books are more specific and less general than the IT books you have seen in the past. Our unique business model allows us to bring you more focused information, giving you more of what you need to know, and less of what you don't.

Packt is a modern, yet unique publishing company, which focuses on producing quality, cutting-edge books for communities of developers, administrators, and newbies alike. For more information, please visit our website: www.packtpub.com.

About Packt Open Source

In 2010, Packt launched two new brands, Packt Open Source and Packt Enterprise, in order to continue its focus on specialization. This book is part of the Packt Open Source brand, home to books published on software built around Open Source licences, and offering information to anybody from advanced developers to budding web designers. The Open Source brand also runs Packt's Open Source Royalty Scheme, by which Packt gives a royalty to each Open Source project about whose software a book is sold.

Writing for Packt

We welcome all inquiries from people who are interested in authoring. Book proposals should be sent to author@packtpub.com. If your book idea is still at an early stage and you would like to discuss it first before writing a formal book proposal, contact us; one of our commissioning editors will get in touch with you.

We're not just looking for published authors; if you have strong technical skills but no writing experience, our experienced editors can help you develop a writing career, or simply get some additional reward for your expertise.

www.ingramcontent.com/pod-product-compliance
Lightning Source LLC
Chambersburg PA
CBHW060151060326
40690CB00018B/4072

* 9 781782 166443 *